Prisoners of P

Women Wage-Workers, Their Tr

Helen Campbell

Alpha Editions

This edition published in 2024

ISBN 9789362513229

Design and Setting By
Alpha Editions
www.alphaedis.com
Email - info@alphaedis.com

Contents

PRISONERS OF POVERTY.

"Make no more giants, God,
But elevate the race at once. We ask
To put forth just our strength, our human strength.
All starting fairly, all equipped alike,
Gifted alike, all eagle-eyed, true-hearted,—
See if we cannot beat Thy angels yet."

"Light, light, and light! to break and melt in sunder
All clouds and chains that in one bondage bind
Eyes, hands, and spirits, forged by fear and wonder
And sleek fierce fraud with hidden knife behind;
There goes no fire from heaven before their thunder,
Nor are the links not malleable that wind
Round the snared limbs and souls that ache thereunder;
The hands are mighty were the head not blind.
Priest is the staff of king,
And chains and clouds one thing,
And fettered flesh with devastated mind.
Open thy soul to see,
Slave, and thy feet are free.
Thy bonds and thy beliefs are one in kind,
And of thy fears thine irons wrought,
Hang weights upon thee fashioned out of thine own thought."

PREFACE.

THE chapters making up the present volume were prepared originally as a series of papers for the Sunday edition of "The New York Tribune," and were based upon minutest personal research into the conditions described. Sketchy as the record may seem at points, it is a photograph from life; and the various characters, whether employers or employed, were all registered in case corroboration were needed. While research was limited to New York, the facts given are much the same for any large city, and thus have a value beyond their immediate application. No attempt at an understanding of the labor question as it faces us to-day can be successful till knowledge of its underlying conditions is assured.

It is such knowledge that the writer has aimed to present; and it takes more permanent form, not only for the many readers whose steady interest has been an added demand for faithful work, but, it is hoped, for a circle yet unreached, who, whether agreeing or disagreeing with the conclusions, still know that to learn the struggle and sorrow of the workers is the first step toward any genuine help.

ORANGE, NEW JERSEY, *March*, 1887.

CHAPTER FIRST.

WORKER AND TRADE.

IN that antiquity which we who only are the real ancients look back upon as the elder world, counting those days as old which were but the beginning of the time we reckon, there were certain methods with workers that centuries ago ceased to have visible form. The Roman matron, whose susceptibilities from long wear and tear in the observation of fighting gladiators and the other mild amusements of the period, were a trifle blunted, felt no compunction in ordering a disobedient or otherwise objectionable slave into chains, and thereafter claiming the same portion of work as had been given untrammelled. The routine of the day demanded certain offices; but how these offices should be most easily fulfilled was no concern of master or mistress, who required simply fulfilment, and wasted no time on consideration of methods. In the homes of Pompeii, once more open to the sun, are the underground rooms where wretched men and women bowed under the weight of fetters, whose corrosion was not only in weary flesh, but in the no less weary soul; and Rome itself can still show the same remnants of long-forgotten wrong and oppression.

That day is over, and well over, we say. Only for a few barbarians still unreached by the march of civilization is any hint of such conditions possible, and even for them the days of darkness are numbered. And so the century moves on; and the few who question if indeed the bonds are quite broken, if civilization has civilized, and if men and women may claim in full their birthright of "life, liberty, and the pursuit of happiness," are set down as hopeless carpers,—unpleasant, pragmatic, generally disagreeable objectors to things as they are. Or if it is admitted that there are defects here and there, and that much remains to be remedied, we are pointed with pride to the magnificent institutions of modern charity, where every possible want of all sorts and conditions of men is met and fulfilled.

"What more would you have?" cries the believer in things as they are. "What is higher or finer than the beautiful spirit that has taken permanent form in brick and mortar? Never since time began has charity been on so magnificent a scale; never has it been so intelligent, so far-seeing. No saints of the past were ever more vowed to good works than these uncanonized saints of to-day who give their lives to the poor and count them well lost. Shame on man or woman who questions the beautiful work or dares hint that under this fair surface rottenness and all foulness still seethe and simmer!"

It is not easy in the face of such feeling to affirm that, perfect as the modern system may be, beautiful as is much of the work accomplished, it still is wanting in one element, the lack of which has power to vitiate the whole. No good-will, no charity, however splendid, fills or can fill the place owned by that need which is forever first and most vital between man and man,—justice. No love, no labor, no self-sacrifice even, can balance that scale in which justice has no place. No knowledge nor wisdom nor any understanding that can come to man counts as force in the universe of God till that one word heads the list of all that must be known and loved and lived before ever the kingdom of heaven can begin upon earth.

It is because this is felt and believed by a few as a compelling power, by many as a dimly comprehended need, so far in the shadow that its form is still unknown, that I begin to-day the search for the real presence. What I write will be no fanciful picture of the hedged-in lives the conditions of which I began, many years ago, to study. If names are withheld, and localities not always indicated, it is not because they are not recorded in full, ready for reference or any required corroboration. Where the facts make against the worker, they are given with as minute detail as where they make against the employer. The one aim in the investigation has been and is to tell the truth simply, directly, and in full, leaving it for the reader to determine what share is his or hers in the evil or in the good that the methods of to-day may hold. That our system of charities and corrections is unsurpassable does not touch the case of the worker who wants no charity and needs no correction. It is something beyond either that must be understood. Till the methods of the day are analyzed, till one has defined justice, asked what claim it makes upon the personal life of man and woman, and mastered every detail that render definition more possible, the questions that perplex even the most conservative can have no solution for this generation or for any generation to come. To help toward such solution is the one purpose of all that will follow.

In the admirable report of the Bureau of Statistics of Labor for 1885, made under the direction of Mr. Charles Peck, whose name is already the synonyme for careful and intelligent work, the number of working-women in New York is given as very nearly two hundred thousand. Investigations of the same nature have been made at other points, notably Boston, in the work of Mr. Carroll D. Wright, one of the most widely known of our statisticians. But neither Boston nor any other city of the United States offers the same facilities or gives as varied a range of employment as is to be found in New York, where grinding poverty and fabulous wealth walk side by side, and where the "life limit" in wages was established long before modern political economy had made the phrase current. This number does not include domestic servants, but is limited to actual handicrafts. Ninety-two trades are given as standing open to women to-day, and several have been added since the report was made. A lifetime would hardly be sufficient for a detailed examination of every industry in the great city, but it is quite possible to form a just judgment of the quality and character of all those which give employment to women. The city which affords the largest percentage of habitual drunkards, as well as the largest number of liquor saloons to the mile, is naturally that in which most women are forced to seek such means of subsistence may be had.

The better-paying trades are filled with women who have had some form of training in school or home, or have passed from one occupation to another, till that for which they had most aptitude has been determined. That, however, to which all the more helpless turn at once, as the one thing about the doing of which there can be no doubt or difficulty, is the one most overcrowded, most underpaid, and with its scale of payments lessening year by year. The girl too ignorant to reckon figures, too dull-witted to learn by observation, takes refuge in sewing in some of its many forms as the one thing possible to all grades of intelligence; and the woman with drunken or otherwise vicious husband, more helpless often than the widow who turns in the same direction, seeks the same sources of employment. If respectably dressed and able to furnish some reference, employment is often found by her in factory or some large establishments where regular workers have place. But if, as is often the case, the need for work arises from the death or the evil habits of the natural head of the family, fortunes have sunk to so low an ebb that often the only clothing left is on the back of the worker, in the last stages of demoralization; and the sole method of securing work is through the middle-men or "sweaters," who ask no questions and require no reference, but make as large a profit for themselves as can be wrung from the helplessness and the bitter need of those with whom they reckon.

The difficulties to be faced by the woman whose only way of self-support is limited to the needle, whether in machine or hand work, fourfold. (1) Her own incompetency must very often head the list and prevent her from securing first-class work; (2) middle-men or sweaters lower the price to starvation point; (3) contract work done in prisons or reformatories brings about the same result; and (4) she is underbid from still another quarter, that of the country woman who takes the work at any price offered.

These conditions govern the character and quality of the work obtained, even the best firms being somewhat affected by the last two clauses. And in every trade there may always be found three distinct classes of employers: the west-side firms, which in many cases care for their workmen, in degree at least, and where the work is done under conditions that must be called favorable; the east-side firms, representing generally cheaper material and lower rates; and last, the slop-work, which may be either east or west, most often the former, and includes every form of outrage and oppression that workers can know.

Clothing in all its multiplied forms takes the first place in the ninety-two trades, and the workers on what is known as "white wear" form the large majority of the always increasing army. For many reasons, the shirt-makers naturally head the list,—the shirt-makers about whom has hung a certain sentimental interest since the day when poor Tom Hood's impassioned plea in their behalf first saw the light. Yet to-day, in spite of popular belief that they are the class most grossly wronged, the shirt-maker fares far better than the majority of the workers on any other form of clothing. This always, however, if she is fortunate enough to have direct relation with some large factory, or with an establishment which gives out the work directly into the hands of the women themselves. Given these conditions, it is possible for a first-class operator to make from seven to twelve dollars per week, the latter sum being certain only in the factories where steam is the motive power and where experience has given the utmost facility in handling the work. In one factory on the west side, employing some one hundred and fifty girls, and where everything had been brought to almost mathematical accuracy, the price paid per dozen for shirts was $2.40. But one of the operatives was able to make a dozen a day, her usual average being about nine, or five dozen per week of sixty hours. Here every condition was exceptionally favorable. The building occupied the centre of a small square, and thus had light on all sides; ventilation was good; and the forewoman, on whose intelligence and good disposition much of the comfort of the operatives depends, was far beyond the average woman in this position. The working day was ten hours, with half an hour for dinner, and the sanitary conditions more favorable than in any other establishment of the same size. Many of the operatives had been there for years, and the dull season, common to all phases of the clothing trade, was never marked enough here to produce discharges or materially lessen production. The wages averaged seven dollars per week, though the laundry women and finishers seldom exceeded five. No middle-men were employed, and none of the customary exactions in the way of fines and other impositions were practised. Piece-work was regarded as the only secure method for both employer and employed, as in such case it rested with the girl herself to make the highest or the lowest rate at pleasure. There were no holidays beyond the legal ones, but all the freedom possible to constant labor was given, the place representing the best conditions of this special industry. Another firm quite as well known and employing equal number of workers had found it more expedient to give up the factory system, and simply retained rooms for cutting and general handling of the completed work, giving it out in packages to workers at home. One woman employed by them for seven years had never made anything but the button-holes in the small piece attached to the bosom, and such fine lettering as was ordered for custom shirts, her wages in the busy season being often twelve dollars a week, the year's average, however, bringing them to seven. She worked exclusively at home, and represented the best paid and most comfortable phase of the industry.

Descending a step, and turning to establishments on the east side, one found every phase of sanitary condition, including under this head bad ventilation, offensive odors, facilities for washing, quality of drinking water, position of water-closets, length of time allowed for lunch, length of working day, etc. Here the quality of the work was lower, material, thread, and sewing being all of an order to be expected from the price of the completed garment, ranging from forty to sixty cents. The wages, however, did not fall so far below the average as might be expected, the operator earning from five to eight dollars a week during the busy season. But the greater number of manufacturers on both east and west sides of the city turn over the work to middle-men, or send it to the country, many factories being run in New Jersey and Pennsylvania, where rents are merely nominal. This proved to be the case with several firms whose names represent a large business, but who find less trouble and more profit in the contract system.

Still another method has gone far toward reducing the rates of payment to the city worker, and this is the giving out the work in packages to the wives and daughters of farmers in the outlying country. These women, having homes, and thus no rent or general expenses to meet, take the work at rates which for the city operators mean simply starvation, and thus prices are kept down, and one more stumbling-block put in the way of the unprotected worker. Careful examination of this phase shows that the applicants, many of whom give assumed names, work simply for the sake of pin-money, which is expended in dress. Now and then it is a case of want, and often that of a woman who, failing to make her husband see that she has any right to an actual cash share in what the work of her own hands has helped to earn, turns to this as the only method of securing some slight personal income. But for the most part, it is only for pin-money; and no argument could convince these earners that their work is in any degree illegitimate or fraught with saddest consequences to those who, because of it, receive just so much the less. Nor would it be possible to bring such argument to bear. To earn seems the inalienable right of any who are willing to work, and the result of methods will never be questioned by employer or employed, unless they are forced to it by more powerful considerations than any at present brought forward.

I have chosen to give these details minutely because they are, practically, the summing up, not only for shirt-making, but for every trade which can be said to come under the head of clothing, whether for men, women, or children,—this including every form of trimming or other adornment used in dress from artificial flowers to gimps, fringes, and buttons. And now, having given this general outline, we may pass to the stories of the units that make up this army,—stories chosen from quarters where doubt is impossible, and confirmed often by the unwilling testimony of those from whom the work has come, giving with them also the necessary details of the trades they may represent, and seeking first, last, and always, only the actual facts that make up the life of the worker.

CHAPTER SECOND.

THE CASE OF ROSE HAGGERTY.

"THE case of Rose Haggerty." So it stands on the little record-book in which long ago certain facts began to have place, each one a count in the indictment of the civilization of to-day, and each one the story not only of Rose but of many another in like case. For the student of conditions among working-women soon discovers that workers divide themselves naturally into four classes: (1) those who have made deliberate choice of a trade, fitted themselves carefully for it, and in time become experts, certain of employment and often of becoming themselves employers; (2) those who by death of relatives or other accident of fortune have been thrown upon their own resources and accept blindly the first means of support that offers, sometimes developing unexpected power and meeting with the same success as the first class; (3) those who have known no other life but that of work, and who accept that to which they most incline with neither energy nor ability enough to rise beyond a certain level; and (4) those who would not work at all save for the pressure of poverty, and who make no effort to gain more knowledge or to improve conditions. But the ebb and flow in this great sea of toiling humanity wipes out all dividing lines, and each class so shades into the next that formal division becomes impossible, but is rather a series of interchanges with no confinement to fixed limits. Often in passing from one trade to another, chance brings about much the same result for each class, and no energy or patience of effort is sufficient to check the inevitable descent into the valley of the shadow, where despair walks forever hand in hand with endeavor.

This time had by no means come for Rose, with just enough of her happy-go-lucky father's nature to make her essentially optimistic. Born in a Cherry Street tenement-house, she had refused to be killed by semi-starvation or foul smells, or dirt of any nature whatsoever. Dennis Haggerty, longshoreman professionally, and doer of all odd jobs in the intervals of his discharges and re-engagements, explained the situation to his own satisfaction, if not to that of Rose and the five other small Haggertys remaining from the brood of twelve.

"If a man wants his dhrink that bad that no matter what he's said overnight he'd sell his soul by the time mornin' comes for even a thimbleful, he's got jist to go to destruction, an' there's no sthoppin' him. An' I've small call to be blamin' Norah whin she comforts herself a bit in the same manner of way, nor will I so long's me name's Dennis Haggerty. But you, Rose, you look out an' get any money you'll find in me pockets, an' keep the children straight, an' all the saints'll see you through the job."

Rose listened, the laugh in her blue eyes shadowed by the sense of responsibility that by seven was fully developed. She did not wonder that her mother drank. Why not, when there was no fire in the stove, and nothing to cook if there had been, and the children counted it a day when they had a scraping of butter on the bread? But, as often happens in these cases, the disgust at smell and taste of liquor grew with every month of her life, and two at least of the children shared it. They were never beaten; for Haggerty at his worst remained good-natured, and when sober wept maudlin tears over his flock and swore that no drop should ever pass his lips again; and Norah echoed every word, and for days perhaps washed and scrubbed and scoured, earning fair wages, and gradually redeeming the clothes or furniture pledged round the corner. Rose went to school when she had anything to wear, and learned in time, when she saw the first symptoms of another debauch, to bundle every wearable thing together and take them and all small properties to the old shoemaker on the first floor, where they remained in hiding till it was safe to produce them again. She had learned this and many another method before the fever which suddenly appeared in early spring took not only her father and mother, but the small Dennis whose career as newsboy had been her pride and delight, and who had been relied upon as half at least of their future dependence. There remained, then, Norah, hopelessly incurable of spinal disease and helpless to move save as Rose lifted her, and the three little ones, as to whose special gifts there was as yet no definite knowledge. In the mean time they were simply three very clamorous mouths to be stopped with such food as might be; and Rose entered a bag-factory a block away, leaving bread and knife and molasses-pitcher by Norah's bed, and trusting the saints to avert disaster from the three experimenting babies. She earned the first month ten dollars, or two and a half a week, but being exceptionally quick, was promoted in the second to four dollars weekly. The rent was six dollars a month; and during the first one the old shoemaker came to the rescue, had an occasional eye to the children, and himself paid the rent, telling Rose to return it when she could. When the ten hours' labor ended, the child, barely fourteen, rushed home to cook something warm for supper, and when the children were comforted and tucked away in the wretched old bed, that still was clean and decent, washed and mended their rags of clothes, and brought such order as she could into the forlorn room.

It was the old shoemaker, a patient, sad-eyed old Scotchman, who also had his story, who settled for her at last that a machine must be had in order that she might work at home. The woman in the room back of his took in shirts from a manufacturer on Division Street, and made often seven and eight dollars a week. She was ready to teach, and in two or three evenings Rose had practically mastered details, and settled that, as she was so young, she would not apply for work in person, but take it through Mrs. Moloney, who would be supposed to have gone into business on her own account as a "sweater." Whatever temptations Mrs. Moloney may have had to make a little profit as "middle-man," she resisted and herself saw that the machine selected was a good one; that no advantage was taken of Rose's inexperience; and that the agent had no opportunity to follow out what had now and then been his method, and hint to the girl that her pretty face entitled her to concessions that would be best made in a private interview. Shame in every possible form and phase had been part of the girl's knowledge since babyhood, but it had slipped away from her, as a foul garment might fall from the fair statue over which it had chanced to be thrown. It was not the innocence of ignorance,—a poor possession at best. It was an ingrained repulsion, born Heaven knows how, and growing as mysteriously with her growth, an invisible yet most potent armor, recognized by every dweller in the swarming tenement. She had her father's quick tongue and laughing eyes, but they could flash as well, and the few who tried a coarse jest shrunk back from both look and scorching word.

Thus far all went well with the poor little fortunes. She worked always ten and twelve, sometimes fourteen, hours a day, yet her strength did not fail, and there was no dearth of work. It was in 1880, and prices were nearly double the present rates. To-day work from the same establishment means not over $4.50 per week, and has even fallen as low as $3.50. In 1880 the shirts were given out by the dozen as at present, going back to the factory to pass through the hands of the finisher and buttonhole maker. The machine operator could make nine of the best class of shirts in a day of ten hours, being paid for them at the rate of $1.75 per dozen. Four spools of cotton, two hundred yards each, were required for a dozen, the price of which must be deducted from the receipts; but the firm preferred to supply twenty-four-hundred-yard spools, at fifty cents for six-cord cotton used for the upper thread, and thirty cents for the three-cord cotton used as under thread, the present prices for same quality and size being respectively forty-five and twenty-five cents. Making nine a day, the week's wages would be for the four dozen and a half $7.87, or $7.50 deducting thread; but Rose averaged five dozen weekly, and for nearly two years counted herself as certain of not less than thirty dollars per month and often thirty-five. The machine had been paid for. The room took on as comfortable a look as its dingy walls and narrow windows would allow; and Bridget, age five, had developed distinct genius for housekeeping, and washed dishes and faces with equal energy and enthusiasm. She did all errands also, and could not be cheated in the matter of change. She knew where the largest loaves were to be had, and sniffed suspiciously at the packets of tea.

"By the time she's seven, she'll do all but the washing," Rose said with pride, and Bridget reverted to childhood for an instant, and spun round on one foot as she made answer:—

"Shure, I could now, if you'd only be lettin' me."

"There's women on the west side that'll earn $2.50 a dozen, for work no better than you're doing now," some one who had come from that quarter said to her one day, but Rose shook her head. There is a curious conservatism among these workers, who cling to familiar haunts and regard unknown regions with suspicion and even terror.

"I've no time for change," Rose said. "It might not be as certain when I'd got it. I'll run no risks;" and she tugged her great bundle of work up the stairs, rejoicing that living so near saved just so much on expressage, a charge paid by the workers themselves.

There were signs well known to the old hands of a probable reduction of prices, weeks before the first cut came. More fault was found. A slipped stitch or a break in the thread was pounced upon with even more promptness than had been their usual portion. Some hands were discharged, and at last came the general cut, resented by some, wailed over by all, but accepted as inevitable. Another, and another, and another followed. Too much production; too many Jew firms competing and under-bidding; more and more foreigners coming in ready to take the work at half price. These reasons and a dozen others of the same order were given glibly, and at first with a certain show of kindliness and attempt to soften harsh facts as much as possible. But the patience of diplomacy soon failed, and questioners of all orders were told that if they did not like it they had nothing to do but to leave and allow a crowd of waiting substitutes to take their places at half rates. The shirt that had sold for seventy-five cents and one dollar had gone down to forty-five and sixty cents respectively, and as cottons and linens had fallen in the same proportion, there was still profit for all but the worker. Here and there were places on Grand or Division Streets where they might even be bought for thirty and forty cents, the price per dozen to the worker being at last from fifty to sixty cents. In the factories it was still possible to earn some approximation to the old rate, but employers had found that it was far cheaper to give out the work; some choosing to give the entire shirt at so much per dozen; others preferring to send out what is known as "team work," flaps being done by one, bosoms by another, and so on.

For a time Rose hemmed shirt-flaps at four cents a dozen, then took first one form and then another of underclothing, the rates on which had fallen in the same proportion, to find each as sure a means of starvation as the last. She had no knowledge of ordinary family sewing, and no means of obtaining such work, had any training fitted her for it; domestic service was equally impossible for the same reason, and the added one that the children must not be left, and she struggled on, growing a little more haggard and worn with every week, but the pretty eyes still holding a gleam of the old merriment. Even that went at last. It was a hard winter. The steadiest work could not give them food enough or warmth enough. The children cried with hunger and shivered with cold. There was no refuge save in Norah's bed, under the ragged quilts; and they cowered there till late in the day, watching Rose as she sat silent at the sewing-machine. There was small help for them in the house. The workers were all in like case, and for the most part drowned their troubles in stale beer from the bucket-shop below.

"Put the children in an asylum, and then you can marry Mike Rooney and be comfortable enough," they said to her, but Rose shook her head.

"I've mothered 'em so far, and I'll see 'em through," she said, "but the saints only knows how. If I can't do it by honest work, there's one way left that's sure, an' I'll try that."

There came a Saturday night when she took her bundle of work, shirts again, and now eighty-five cents a dozen. There were five dozen, and when the $1.50 was laid aside for rent it was easy to see what remained for food, coal, and light. Clothing had ceased to be part of the question. The children were barefoot. They had a bit of meat on Sundays, but for the rest, bread, potatoes, and tea were the diet, with a cabbage and bit of pork now and then for luxuries. Norah had been failing, and to-night Rose planned to buy her "something with a taste to it," and looked at the sausages hanging in long links with a sudden reckless determination to get enough for all. She was faint with hunger, and staggered as she passed a basement restaurant, from which came savory smells, snuffed longingly by some half-starved children. Her turn was long in coming, and as she laid her bundle on the counter she saw suddenly that her needle had "jumped," and that half an inch or so of a band required resewing. As she looked the foreman's knife slipped under the place, and in a moment half the band had been ripped.

"That's no good," he said. "You're getting botchier all the time."

"Give it to me," Rose pleaded. "I'll do it over."

"Take it if you like," he said indifferently, "but there's no pay for that kind o' work."

He had counted her money as he spoke, and Rose cried out as she saw the sum.

"Do you mean you'll cheat me of the whole dozen because half an inch on one is gone wrong?"

"Call it what you like," he said. "R. & Co. ain't going to send out anything but first-class work. Stand out of the way and let the next have a chance. There's your three dollars and forty cents."

Rose went out silently, choking down rash words that would have lost her work altogether, but as she left the dark stairs and felt again the cutting wind from the river, she stood still, something more than despair on her face. The children could hardly fare worse without her than with her. The river could not be colder than this cold world that gave her no chance, and that had no place for anything but rascals. She turned toward it as the thought came, but some one had her arm, and she cried out suddenly and tried to wrench away.

"Easy now," a voice said. "You're breakin' your heart for trouble, an' here I am in the nick o' time. Come with me an' you'll have no more of it, for my pocket's full to-night, an' that's more 'n it'll be in the mornin' if you don't take me in tow."

It was a sailor from a merchantman just in, and Rose looked at him for a moment. Then she took his arm and walked with him toward Roosevelt Street.

It might be dishonor, but it was certainly food and warmth for the children, and what did it matter? She had fought her fight for twenty years, and it had been a vain struggle. She took his money when morning came, and went home with the look that is on her face to-day.

"I'll marry you out of hand," the sailor said to her; but Rose answered, "No man alive'll ever marry me after this night," and she has kept her word. She has her trade, and it is a prosperous one, in which wages never fail. The children are warm and have no need to cry for hunger any more.

"It's not a long life we live," Rose says quietly. "My kind die early, but the children will be well along, an' all the better when the time comes that they've full sense for not having to know what way the living comes. But let God Almighty judge who's to blame most—I that was driven, or them that drove me to the pass I'm in."

CHAPTER THIRD.

SOME METHODS OF A PROSPEROUS FIRM.

"THE emancipation of women is certainly well under way, when all underwear can be bought more cheaply than it is possible to make it up at home, and simple suits of very good material make it hardly more difficult for a woman to clothe herself without thought or worry, than it has long been for a man."

This was the word heard at a woman's club not long ago, and reinforced within the week by two well-known journals edited in the interests of women at large. The editorial page of one held a fervid appeal for greater simplicity of dress and living in general, followed by half a column of entreaty to women to buy ready-made clothing, and thus save time for higher pursuits and the attainment of broader views. With feebler pipe, but in the same key, sounded the second advocate of simplification, adding:—

"Never was there a time when women could dress with as much real elegance on as small an expenditure of money. Bargains abound, and there is small excuse for dowdiness. The American woman is fast taking her place as the best-dressed woman in the civilized world."

Believing very ardently that the right of every woman born includes not only "life, liberty, and the pursuit of happiness," but beauty also, it being one chief end of woman to include in her own personality all beauty attainable by reasonable means, I am in heartiest agreement with one side of the views quoted. But in this quest we have undertaken, and from which, once begun, there is no retreat, strange questions arise; and in this new dawn of larger liberty and wider outlook is seen the little cloud which, if no larger than a man's hand, holds the seed of as wild a storm as has ever swept over humanity.

For emancipation on the one side has meant no corresponding emancipation for the other; and as one woman selects, well pleased, garment after garment, daintily tucked and trimmed and finished beyond any capacity of ordinary home sewing, marvelling a little that a few dollars can give such lavish return, there arises, from narrow attic and dark, foul basement, and crowded factory, the cry of the women whose life-blood is on these garments. Through burning, scorching days of summer; through marrow-piercing cold of winter, in hunger and rags, with white-faced children at their knees, crying for more bread, or, silent from long weakness, looking with blank eyes at the flying needle, these women toil on, twelve, fourteen, sixteen hours even, before the fixed task is done. The slice of baker's bread and the bowl of rank black tea, boiled to extract every possibility of strength, are taken, still at the machine. It is easier to sit there than in rising and movement to find what weariness is in every limb. There is always a child old enough to boil the kettle and run for a loaf of bread; and all share the tea, which gives a fictitious strength, laying thus the foundation for the fragile, anæmic faces and figures to be found among the workers in the bag-factories, paper-box manufactories, etc.

"Why don't they go into the country?" is often asked. "Why do they starve in the city when good homes and ample pay are waiting for them?"

It is not with the class to whom this question is applicable that we deal to-day. Of the army of two hundred thousand who battle for bread, nearly a third have no resource but the needle, and of this third many thousands are widows with children, to whom they cling with a devotion as strong as wiser mothers feel, and who labor night and day to prevent the scattering into asylums, and consequent destruction of the family as a family. They are widows through many causes that can hardly be said to come under the head of "natural." Drunkenness leads, and the thousand accidents that are born of drunkenness, but there are other methods arising from the same greed that underlies most modern civilization. The enormous proportion of accidents, which, if not killing instantly, imply long disability and often death as the final result, come nine tenths of the time from criminal disregard of any ordinary means of protecting machinery. One great corporation, owning thousands of miles of railroad, saw eight hundred men disabled in greater or less degree in one year, and still refused to adopt a method of coupling cars which would have saved the lives of the sixty-eight brakemen who were sacrificed to the instinct of economy dominating the superintendent. The same man refused to roof over a spot where a number of freight-handlers were employed during a stormy season, rheumatism and asthma being the consequences for many, and his reason had at least the merit of frankness,—a merit often lacking in explanations that, even when most plausible, cover as essential a brutality of nature.

"Men are cheaper than shingles," he said. "There's a dozen waiting to fill the place of one that drops out."

In another case, in a great saw-mill, the owner had been urged to protect a lath-saw, swearing at the persistent request, even after the day when one of his best men was led out to the ambulance, his right hand hanging by a bit of skin, his death from lockjaw presently leaving one more widow to swell the number. It is of such men that a sturdy thinker wrote last year, "Man is a self-damnable animal," and it is on such men that the curse of the worker lies heaviest. That they exist at all is hardly credited by the multitude who believe that, for this country at least, oppression and outrage are only names. That they exist in numbers will be instantly denied; yet to one who has heard the testimony given by weeping women, and confirmed by the reluctant admissions of employers themselves, there comes belief that no words can fully tell what wrong is still possible from man to man in this America, the hope of nations.

Is this a digression hardly to be pardoned in a paper on the trades and lives of women,—a deliberate turning toward an issue which has neither place nor right in such limits? On the contrary, it is all part of the same wretched story. The chain that binds humanity in one has not one set of links for men and another for women; and the blow aimed at one is felt also not only by those nearest, but by successive ranks to whom the shock, though only by indirect transmission, is none the less deadly in effect. And thus the wrong done on the huge scale appropriate to a great corporation finds its counterpart in a lesser but quite as well organized a wrong, born also of the spirit of greed, and working its will as pitilessly.

"If you employed on a large scale you would soon find that you ceased to look at your men as men," said an impatient iron-worker not long ago. "They are simply so much producing power. I don't propose to abuse them, but I've no time even to remember their faces, much less their names."

Precisely on this principle reasons the employer of women, who are even less to be regarded as personalities than men. For the latter, once a year at least the employer becomes conscious of the fact that these masses of "so much producing power" are resolvable into votes, and on election day, if on no other, worthy of analysis. There is no such necessity in the case of women. The swarming crowd of applicants are absolutely at the mercy of the manager or foreman, who, unless there is a sudden pressure of work, makes the selections according to fancy, youth and any gleam of prettiness being unfailing recommendations. There are many firms of which this could not be said with any justice. There are many more in which it is the law, tacitly laid down, but none the less a fact. With such methods of selection go other methods supposed to be confined to the lowest grade of work and the lowest type of employer, both being referred to regions like Baxter or Division Streets. But they are to be found east or west indifferently, the illustration at present in mind being on Canal Street, within sound of Broadway. It is a prosperous firm, one whose trade-mark can be trusted; and here are a few of the methods by which this prosperity has been attained, and goes on in always-increasing ratio.

In the early years of their existence as a firm they manufactured on the premises, but, like many other firms, found that it was a very unnecessary expense. A roof over the heads of a hundred or more women, with space for their machines, meant not less than twenty-five hundred dollars a year to be deducted from the profits. Even floors in some cheaper quarter were still an expense to be avoided if possible. The easy way out of the difficulty was to make the women themselves pay the rent, not in any tangible imposition of tax, but none the less certainly in fact. Nothing could be simpler. Manufacturing on the premises had only to cease, and it could even be put as a favor to the women that they were allowed to work at home. The rule established itself at once, and the firm, smiling serenely at the stoppage of this most damaging and most unnecessary leak, proceeded to make fresh discoveries of equally satisfactory possibilities. To each woman who applied for work it was stated:—

"We send all packages from the cutting-room by express, the charges to be paid by you. It's a small charge, only fifteen cents, to be paid when the bundle comes in."

"We can come for ours. We live close by. We don't want to lose the fifteen cents," a few objected, but the answer was invariable:—

"It suits us best to make up the packages in the cutting-room, and if you don't like the arrangement there are plenty waiting that it will suit well enough."

Plenty waiting! How well they knew it, and always more and more as the ships came in, and the great tide of "producing power" flowed through Castle Garden, and stood, always at high-water mark, in the wards where cheap labor may be found. Plenty waiting; and these women who could not wait went home and turned over their small store of pennies for the fifteen cents, the payment of which meant either a little less bread or an hour or two longer at the sewing-machine, defined as the emancipator of women.

In the mean time the enterprising firm had made arrangements with a small express company to deliver the packages at twelve cents each, and could thus add to the weekly receipts a clear gain of three cents per head. It is unnecessary to add that they played into each other's hands, and that the wagon-drivers had no knowledge of anything beyond the fact that they were to collect the fifteen cents and turn it over to their superiors. But in some manner it leaked out; and a driver whose feelings had been stirred by the sad face of a little widow on Sixth Street told her that the fifteen cents was "a gouge," and they had all better put their heads together and refuse to pay more than twelve cents.

"If we had any heads, it might do to talk about putting them together," the little widow said bitterly. "For my part, I begin to believe women are born fools, but I'll see what I can do."

This "seeing" involved earning a dollar or two less for the week, but the cheat seemed so despicable a one that indignation made her reckless, and she went to the woman who had first directed her to the firm and had been in its employ almost from the beginning.

"It's like 'em; oh, yes, it's like 'em!" she said, "but we've no time to spend in stirring up things, and you know well enough what would be the end of it if we did,—discharged, and somebody else getting our wages. You'd better not talk too much if you want to keep your place."

"That isn't any worse than the thread dodge," another woman said. "I know from a clerk in the house where they buy their thread, that they charge us five cents a dozen more than it costs them, though they make a great point of giving it to us at cost and cheaper than we could buy it ourselves."

"Why don't you club together and buy, then?" the little widow asked, to hear again the formula, "And get your walking-ticket next day? We know a little better than that."

A few weeks later a new system of payment forced each worker to sacrifice from half an hour to an hour of precious time, her only capital. Hitherto payments had been made at the desk when work was brought in, but now checks were given on a Bowery bank, and the women must walk over in heat and storm alike, and wait their turn in the long line on the benches. If paid by the week this would make little difference, as any loss of time would be the employers', but this form of payment is practically abolished, piece-work done at home meaning the utmost amount of profit to the employer, every loss in time being paid by the workers themselves. When questioned as to why the check system of payment had been adopted by this and various other firms, the reply was simply:—

"It saves trouble. The bank has more time to count out money than we have."

"But the women? Does it seem quite fair that they should be the losers?"

"Fair? Anything's fair in business. You'd find that out if you undertook to do it."

As the case then at present stands, for this firm, and for many which have adopted the same methods, the working-woman not only pays the rent that would be required for a factory, but gives them a profit on expressage, thread, time lost in going to bank, and often the price on a dozen of garments, payment for the dozen being deducted by many foremen if there is a flaw in one. This foreman becomes the scapegoat if unpleasant questions are asked by any whose investigation might bring discredit on the firm. In some cases they refuse positively to give any information, but in most, questions are answered with suspicious glibness, and if reference is made to any difficulties encountered by the women in their employ, they take instant refuge in the statement:—

"Oh, that was before the last foreman left. We discharged him as soon as we found out how he had served the women."

"Do you see those goods?" another asked, pointing to a counter filled with piles of chemises. "How do you suppose we make a cent when you can buy a chemise like that for fifty cents? We don't. The competition is ruining us, and we're talking of giving up the business."

"That's so. It's really more in charity to the women than anything else that we go on," his partner remarked, with a look toward him which seemed to hold a million condensed winks. "That price is just ruin; that's what it is."

Undoubtedly, but not for the firm, as the following figures will show,— figures given by a competent forewoman in a large establishment where she had had eleven years' experience: twenty-seven yards and three-quarters are required for one dozen chemises, the price paid for such cotton as is used in one selling at fifty cents being five cents per yard, or $1.40 for the whole amount; thirty yards of edging at 4½ cents a yard furnishes trimming for the dozen, at $1.35; and four two-hundred-yard spools of cotton are required, at twenty-five cents per dozen, or eight cents per dozen garments. The seamer who sews up and hems the bodies of the garments receives thirty cents a dozen, and the "maker"—this being the technical term for the more experienced worker who puts on band and sleeves—receives from ninety cents to one dollar a dozen, though at present the rates run from seventy-five to ninety cents. Our table, then, stands as follows:—

Cloth for one dozen chemises	$1.40
Edging " "	1.35
Thread " "	.08
Seamer " "	.30
Maker " "	.90
Total cost of dozen	$4.03
Wholesale price per dozen	5.25

The chemise which sells at seven dollars per dozen has the additional value in quality of cloth and edging, the same price being paid the work-women, this price varying only in very slight degree till the excessively elaborate work demanded by special orders. One class of women in New York, whose trade has been a prosperous one since ever time began, pay often one hundred dollars a dozen for the garments, which are simply a mass of lace and cobweb cambric, tucked and puffed, and demanding the highest skill of the machine operator, who even in such case counts herself happy if she can make eight or nine dollars a week. And if any youth and comeliness remain to her, why need there be wonder if the question frame itself: "Why am I the maker of this thing, earning barest living, when, if I choose, I, too, can be buyer and wearer and live at ease?"

Wonder rather that one remains honest when the only thing that pays is vice.

For the garments of lowest grade to be found in the cheapest quarters of the city the price ranges from twenty-five to thirty cents, the maker receiving only thirty cents a dozen, and cloth, trimming, and thread being of the lowest quality. The profit in such case is wellnigh imperceptible; but for the class of employer who secures it, content to grovel in foul streets, and know no joy of living save the one delight of seeing the sordid gains roll up into hundreds of thousands, it is still profit, and he is content. As I write, an evening paper containing the advertisement of a leading dry-goods firm is placed before me, and I read: "Chemises, from 12½ cents up." Here imagination stops. No list of cost prices within my reach tells me how this is practicable. But one thing is certain. Even here it is not the employer who loses; and if it is a question of but a third of a cent profit, be sure that that profit is on his side, never on the side of the worker.

CHAPTER FOURTH.

THE BARGAIN COUNTER.

THE problem of the last chapter is, if not plain, at least far plainer than when it left the pen, and it has become possible to understand how the garment sold at twelve and a half cents may still afford its margin of profit. It has also been made plain that that profit is, as there stated, "never on the side of the worker," but that it is wrung from her by the sharpest and most pitiless of all the methods known to unscrupulous men and the women who have chosen to emulate them. For it has been my evil fortune in this quest to find women not only as filled with greed and as tricky and uncertain in their methods as the worst class of male employers, but even more ingenious in specific modes of imposition. Without exception, so far as I can discover, they have been workers themselves, released for a time it may be by marriage, but taking up the trade again, either from choice or necessity. They have learned every possibility of cheating. They know also far better than men every possibility of nagging, and as they usually own a few machines they employ women on their own premises and keep a watchful eye lest the smallest advantage be gained. The majority prefer to act as "sweaters," this releasing them from the uncertainties attending the wholesale manufacturer, and as the work is given to them at prices at or even below the "life limit," it is not surprising that those to whom they in turn pass it on find their percentage to mean something much nearer death than life.

"Only blind eyes could have failed to see all this before," some reader is certain to say. "How is it possible that any one dealing directly with the question could doubt for a moment the existence of this and a thousand-fold worse fraud?"

Only possible from the same fact that makes these papers a necessity. They hold only new phases of the old story. The grain has had not one threshing alone, but many, and yet for the most patient and persistent of searchers after truth is ever fresh surprise at its nature and extent. Given one or a dozen exposures of a fraud, and we settle instinctively into the conviction that its power has ended. It is barely conceivable to the honest mind that cheating has wonderful staying power, and that not one nor a thousand exposures will turn into straight paths feet used to crooked ones. And when a business man, born to all good things and owning a name known as the synonyme of the best the Republic offers to-day, states calmly, "There is no such thing as business without lying," what room remains for honor or justice or humanity among men whose theory is the same, and who can gild it with no advantage of birth or training? It is a wonderful century, and we are civilizing with a speed that takes away the breath and dims the vision, but there are dark corners still, and in the shadow Greed and Corruption and Shame hold high carnival, with nameless shapes, before which even civilization cowers. Their trace is found at every turn, but we deal with only one to-day, helpless, even when face to face, to say what method will most surely mean destruction.

We settle so easily into the certainty that nothing can be as bad as it seems, that moments of despair come to all who would rouse men to action. Not one generation nor many can answer the call sounding forever in the ears of every son of man; but he who has heeded has at least made heeding more possible for those that follow; and the time comes at last when the way must be plain for all. To make it plainer many a popular conviction must be laid aside, and among them the one that follows.

It is a deeply rooted belief that the poor understand and feel for the poor beyond any possibility in those who have never known cold and hunger and rags save as uncomfortable terms used too freely by injudicious agitators. Like many another popular belief the groundwork is in the believer's own mind, and has its most tangible existence in story-books. There are isolated cases always of self-sacrifice and compassion and all gentle virtues, but long experience goes to show that if too great comfort is deadening, too little is brutalizing, and that pity dies in the soul of man or woman to whom no pity has been shown. It is easy to see, then, how the woman who has found injustice and oppression the law of life, deals in the same fashion when her own time comes, and tyrannizes with the comfortable conviction that she is by this means getting even with the world. She knows every sore spot, and how best to make the galled jade wince, and lightens her own task by the methods practised in the past upon herself. This is one species to be dealt with, and a far less dangerous one than the craftier and less outspokenly brutal order, just above her in grade. It is by these last that some of the chief frauds on women are perpetrated, and here we find one source of the supplies that furnish the bargain counters.

We read periodically of firms detected in imposing upon women, and are likely to feel that such exposure has ended their career as firms once for all. In every trade will be found one or more of these, whose methods of obtaining hands are fraudulent, and who advertise for "girls to learn the trade," with no intention of retaining them beyond the time in which they remain content to work without pay. There are a thousand methods of evasion, even when the law faces them and the victim has made formal complaint. As a rule she is too ignorant and too timid for complaint or anything but abject submission, and this fact is relied upon as certain foundation for success. But, if determined enough, the woman has some redress in her power. Within a few years, after long and often defeated attempts, the Woman's Protective Union has brought about legislation against such fraud, and any employer deliberately withholding wages is liable to fifteen days' imprisonment and the costs of the suit brought against him, a fact of which most of them seem to be still quite unaware. This law, so far as imprisonment is concerned, has no application to women, and they have learned how to evade the points which might be made to bear upon them, by hiring rooms, machines, etc., and swearing that they have no personal property that can be levied upon. Or, if they have any, they transfer it to some friend or relative, as in the case of Madame M——, a fashionable dressmaker notorious for escaping from payment seven times out of ten. She has accumulated money enough to become the owner of a large farm on Long Island, but so ingeniously have all her arrangements been made that it is impossible to make her responsible, and her case is used at the Union as a standing illustration of the difficulty of circumventing a woman bent upon cheating.

A firm, a large proportion of whose goods are manufactured in this manner, can well afford to stock the bargain counters of popular stores. They can afford also to lose slightly by work imperfectly done, though, even with learners, this is in smaller proportion than might be supposed. The girl who comes in answer to their advertisement is anxious to learn the trade at once, and gives her best intelligence to mastering every detail. Her first week is likely to hold an energy of effort that could hardly last, and she can often be beguiled by small payments and large promises to continue weeks and even months, always expecting the always delayed payment. Firms dealing in such fashion change their quarters often, unless in league with police captains who have been given sufficient reasons for obliviousness of their methods, and who have also been known to silence timid complaints with the threat of a charge of theft. But there is always a multitude ready to be duped, and no exposure seems sufficient to prevent this, and women who have once established a business on this system seem absolutely reckless as to any possible consequences.

There is at present on Third Avenue a Mrs. F——, who for eleven years has conducted a successful business built upon continuous fraud. She is a manufacturer of underwear, and the singular fact is that she has certain regular employees who have been with her from the beginning, and who, while apparently unconscious of her methods, are practically partners in the fraud. She is a woman of good presence and address, and one to whom girls submit unquestioningly, contending, even in court, that she never meant to cheat them; and it is still an open question with those who know her best how far she herself recognizes the fraud in her system. The old hands deny that it is her custom to cheat, and though innumerable complaints stand against her, she has usually paid on compulsion, and insisted that she always meant to. Her machines never lack operators, and the grade of work turned out is of the best quality. Her advertisement appears at irregular intervals, is answered by swarms of applicants, and there are always numbers waiting their turn. On a side street a few blocks distant is a deep basement, crowded with machines and presided over by a woman with many of her personal characteristics. It is the lowest order of slop work that is done here, but it helps to fill the bargain counters of the poorer stores, and the workers are an always shifting quantity. It is certain that both places are practically the property of Mrs. F——, but no man has yet been cunning enough to determine once for all her responsibility, and no law yet framed covers any ground that she has chosen as her own. Her prototypes are to be found in every trade open to women, and their numbers grow with the growth of the great city and strengthen in like proportion. The story of one is practically the story of all. Popularly supposed to be a method of trickery confined chiefly to Jews, investigation shows that Americans must share the odium in almost as great degree, and that the long list includes every nationality known to trade.

We have dealt thus far with fraud as the first and chief procurer for bargain counters. Another method results from a fact that thus far must sum up as mainly Jewish. Till within very little more than a year, a large dry-goods firm on the west side employed many women in its underwear department. The work was piece-work, and done by the class of women who own their own machines and work at home. Prices were never high, but the work was steady and the pay prompt. The firm for a time made a specialty of "Mother Hubbard" night-gowns, for which they paid one dollar a dozen for "making," this word covering the making and putting in of yoke and sleeves, the "seamer" having in some cases made the bodies at thirty cents a dozen. Many of the women, however, made the entire garment at $1.30 per dozen, ten being the utmost number practicable in a day of fourteen hours. Suddenly the women were informed that their services would not be required longer. An east-side firm bearing a Jewish name had contracted to do the same work at eighty cents a dozen, and all other underwear in the same proportions. Steam had taken the place of foot-power, and the women must find employment with firms who were willing to keep to slower methods. Necessarily these are an always lessening minority. Competition in this race for wealth crushes out every possibility of thought for the worker save as so much producing power, and what hand and foot cannot do steam must. In several cases in this special manufacture the factories have been transferred to New Jersey and Pennsylvania, where rent is a mere song, and where girls flock in from the adjacent country, eager for the work that represents something higher than either ordinary mill work or the household service they despise.

"What can we do?" said one manufacturer lately, when asked how he thought the thing would end. "If there were any power quicker than steam, or any way of managing so that women could feed five or six machines, that would have to come next, else every one of us would go to the wall together, the pressure is so tremendous. Of course there's no chance for the women, but then you must remember there's precious little chance for the employer either. This competition is a sort of insanity. It gluts the market with cheap goods, and gives a sense of prosperity, but it is the death of all legitimate, reasonable business. It won't surprise me if this whole trade of manufacturing underwear becomes a monopoly, and one man— like O'H——, for instance—swallows up the whole thing. Lord help the women then, for there'll be no help in man!"

"Suppose co-operation were tried? What would be the effect?"

"No effect, because there isn't confidence enough anywhere to make men dare a co-operative scheme. Even the workers would distrust it, and a sharp business man laughs in your face if you mention the word. It doesn't suit American notions. It might be a good thing if there were any old-fashioned business men left,—men content with slow profits and honest dealing,—as my father was, for instance. But he wouldn't have a ghost of a chance to-day. The whole system of business is rotten, and there will have to be a reconstruction clean from the bottom, though it's the men that need it first. We're the maddest nation for money on the face of the earth, and the race is a more killing one every year. I'm half inclined to think sometimes that mankind will soon be pretty much a superfluity, the machines are getting so intelligent; and it may be these conditions that seem to upset you so are simply means of killing off those that are not wanted, and giving place to a less sensitive order of beings. Lord help them, I say again, for there's no help in man."

The speaker nodded, as if this rather unexpected flight of imagination was an inspiration in which might lie the real solution of all difficulties, and hurried away to his waiting niche in the great competitive system. And as he went, there came to me words spoken by one of the workers, in whose life hope was dead, and who also had her theory of any future under to-day's conditions:—

"I've worked eleven years. I've tried five trades with my needle and machine. My shortest day has been fourteen hours, for I had the children and they had to be fed. There's not one of these trades that I don't know well. It isn't work that I've any trouble in getting. It's wages. Five years ago

I could earn $1.50 a day, and we were comfortable. Then it began to go down,—$1.25, then $1.00. There it stopped awhile, and I got used to that, and could even get some remains of comfort out of it. I had to plan to the last half cent. We went cold often, but we were never hungry. But then it fell again,—to ninety cents, to eighty-five. For a year the best that I can do I have earned not over eighty cents a day,—sometimes only seventy-five. I'm sixty-two years old. I can't learn new ways. I am strong. I always was strong. I run the machine fourteen hours a day, with just the stoppings that have to be to get the work ready. I've never asked a man alive for a penny beyond what my own hands can earn, and I don't want it. I suppose the Lord knows what it all means. It's His world and His children in it, and I've kept myself from going crazy many a time by saying it was His world and that somehow it must all come right in the end. But I don't believe it any more. He's forgotten. There's nothing left but men that live to grind the face of the poor; that chuckle when they find a new way of making a cent or two more a week out of starving women and children. I never thought I should feel so; I don't know myself; but I tell you I'm ready for murder when I think of these men. If there's no justice above, it isn't quite dead below; and if men with money will not heed, the men and the women without money will rise some day. How? I don't know. We've no time to plan, and we're too tired to think, but it's coming somehow, and I'm not ashamed to say I'll join in if I live to see it come. It's seas of tears that these men sail on. It's our life-blood they drink and our flesh that they eat. God help them if the storm comes, for there'll be no help in man."

Employer and employed had ended in wellnigh the same words; but the gulf between no words have spanned, and it widens day by day.

CHAPTER FIFTH.

A FASHIONABLE DRESSMAKER.

"COME now, be reasonable, won't you? You've got to move on, you know, and why don't you do it?"

"I'm that reasonable that a bench of judges couldn't be more so; and I'll not move on for anything less than dynamite, and I ain't sure I would for that. It's only a choice between starvation and going into the next world in little bits, and I don't suppose it makes much difference which way it's done."

The small, pale, dogged-looking little woman who announced this conviction did not even rise from the steps where she sat looking up to the big policeman, who faced her uneasily, half turning as if he would escape the consequences of rash action if he knew how. Nothing could be more mysterious. For it was within sight of Broadway, on one of the best-known side streets near Union Square, where business signs were few and of the most decorous order, and where before one door, bearing the name of one of the best-known fashionable dressmakers, a line of carriages stood each day during the busy season. A name hardly less known was on the door-plate of the great house before which she sat, and which still bore every mark of prosperous ownership, while from one of the windows looked the elaborately dressed head of Madame herself, the anxiety in her eyes contradicting the scornful smile on her thin lips. The door just beyond No. — opened, and a stout gentleman descended one step and stood eying the policeman belligerently. That official looked up the street as if wishing for cry of "murder" or "stop thief" around the corner, but hearing neither, concentrated again on the antagonist whose irregular methods defied precedent and gave him a painful sense of insecurity. If two could listen, why not three?—and I paused near the steps, eyed considerately by the stout gentleman, who was evidently on the outlook for allies. A look of intelligence passed between Madame and the policeman, and her head disappeared from the window, a blind on the second story moving slightly and announcing a moment later that she had taken a less conspicuous post of observation.

"Move on now, I tell you!" began the policeman again, but paused, for as he spoke a slender, bright-eyed girl came swiftly toward them, and paused on the first step with a glance of curiosity at the little group.

"Have you come to answer Madame M——'s advertisement?" the little woman said, as she rose from the steps and laid her hand detainingly on the hurrying figure.

"Yes," the girl answered hesitatingly, pulling away from the hand that held.

"Then, unless you've got anything else to do and like to give your time and strength for naught, keep away. You'll get no wages, no matter what's promised. I've been there six months, kept on by fair promises, and I know. I'll let no girl go in there without warning."

"It's a good-looking place," the girl said doubtfully.

"It's a den of thieves all the same. If you don't believe me, come down to the Woman's Protective Union on Clinton Place, and you'll see my case on the book there, and judgment against this woman, that's no more mercy than a Hottentot and lies that smoothly that she'd humbug an angel of light. Ah! that's good!" she added, for the girl had shaken off her hand and sped away as swiftly as she had come. "That's seven since yesterday, and I wish it were seven hundred. It's time somebody turned watchdog."

"That ain't your business. That's a matter for the law," said the big policeman, who had glanced anxiously up to the second-story window and then looked reassured and serene, as the stout gentleman made a significant movement, which indicated that bribery was as possible for one sex as for the other. "The law'll straighten out anything that you've a mind to have it."

"The law! Lord help them that think the law is going to see them through," the small woman said, with a fierceness that made the big policeman start and lay his hand on his club. "What's the law worth when it can't give to you one dollar of two hundred and eight that's owed; and she that earned them gasping her life out with consumption? If it was my account alone do you suppose I'd care? Mine's eighty-five, and I went to law for it, to find she'd as long a head as she has smooth tongue, and had fixed things so that there wasn't a stick of furniture nor a dollar of property that could be levied on. If she'd been a man the new law that gives a cheating employer fifteen days' imprisonment might have worked with her as it's worked with many a rascal that never knew he could be brought up with a round turn. But she's a woman and she slides through, and a judgment against her isn't worth the paper it's written on. So as I can't take it out in money I take it out in being even with her. There are the papers that show I don't lie, and here I sit the time I've fixed to sit, and if she gets the three new hands she's after, it won't be because I haven't done what came to me to do to hinder it."

The policeman had moved away before the words ended, the stout gentleman having descended the steps for a moment, and stood in a position which rendered his little transaction feasible and almost invisible. He beckoned to me as the small woman sat down again on the steps, and I followed him into the vestibule.

"You're interested, my dear madam," he said. "You're interested, and you ought to be. I've stayed home from business to make sure she wasn't interfered with, and I'd do it again with the greatest pleasure. I'd like to post one like her before every establishment in New York where cheating goes on, and I'm going to see this thing through!"

There was no time for questions. My appointment must be kept, and with one pause to take the name and number of the small Nemesis I went my way. Three days later she sat there still, and on the following one, as the warm spring rain fell steadily, she kept her post, sheathed in a rubber cloak, and protected by an umbrella which, from its size and quality, I felt must be the stout gentleman's. With Saturday night her self-imposed siege ended, and she marched away, leaving the enemy badly discomfited and much more disposed to consider the rights of the individual, if not of the worker in general. As Madame's prices were never less than fifty dollars for the making of a suit, ranging from this to a hundred or more, and as her three children were still small and her husband an undiscoverable factor, it became an interesting question to know where she placed the profits which, even when lessened by non-paying customers, could never be anything but great. Madame, however, had been too keen even for the sharp-witted lawyer of the Protective Union, whose utmost efforts only disclosed the fact that she was the probable backer of a manufacturer whose factory and farm were on Long Island, and whose business capacity had till within a few years never insured him more than a bare living.

It is an old story, yet an always new one, and in this case Madame had quieted her conscience by providing a comfortable lunch for the workers and allowing them more space than is generally the portion in a busy establishment. Well housed and well fed through the day and paid at intervals enough to meet the demands of rent or board bill, it was easy to satisfy her hands by the promise of full and speedy settlement, and when this failed, to tell a pitiful tale of unpaid bills and conscienceless customers, who could not be forced. When these resources were exhausted discharge solved any further difficulties, and a new set came in, to undergo the same experience. In an establishment where honesty has any place, the wages are rather beyond the average, skirt-hands receiving from seven to nine dollars a week and waist-hands from ten to fifteen. In the case of stores this latter class make from eighteen to forty dollars per week, and often accumulate enough capital to start in business for themselves. But a skirt-hand like Mary M—— seldom passes on to anything higher, and counts herself well paid if her week of sixty hours brings her nine dollars, not daring to grumble seriously if it falls to seven or even six. On the east side the same work must be done for from four to six dollars a week, the latter sum being considered high pay. But the work is an advance upon factory work and has a better sound, the dressmaker's assistant looking down upon the factory hand or even the seamstress as of an inferior order.

In time I learned the full story of the little woman, ordinarily reticent and shrinking, but brought by trouble and indignation to the fiercest protest against oppression. Born in a New-England village she had learned a milliner's trade, to which she presently added dressmaking, and succeeded in making a fair living, till bitten by the desire to see larger life and share all the good that the city seems to offer the shut-in country life, she came to New York with her small savings, expecting to find work easily, and did so, going at once into a store where a friend was at work. Sanitary conditions were all bad. Her hall bedroom on a fourth floor and the close confinement all did their work, and a long illness wasted strength and savings. When recovery came her place had been filled; and she wandered from store to store seeking employment, doing such odd jobs as were found at intervals, and powerless to recover the lost ground.

"It was like heaven to me," she said, "when my friend came back to the city and got me that place as skirt-hand at Madame M——'s. I was so far gone I had even thought of the river, and said to myself it might be the easiest way out. You can't help but like Madame, for she's smooth-tongued and easy, and praises your work, and she made me think I'd soon be advanced and get the place I ought to have. She paid regularly at first, and I began to pick up courage. It was over-hours always. Madame would come in smiling and say: 'Ah, dear girls! What trouble! It is an order that must be finished so soon. Who will be kind and stay so leetle longer?' Then we all stayed, and she'd have tea made and send it in, and sandwiches or something good, and they all said, 'She's an angel. You won't find anybody like Madame.' She was so plausible, too, that even when there was longer and longer time between the payments the girls didn't blame her, but borrowed of one another and put off their landladies and managed all ways to save her feelings. Jenny G—— had been here longer than any of them, and she worshipped Madame and wouldn't hear a word even when one or another complained. But Jenny's feet were on the ground and she hadn't a stitch of warm underclothes, and she took a cold in December, and by January it had tight hold of her. I went to Madame myself then, and begged her to pay Jenny if it wasn't but a little, and she cried and said if she could only raise the money she would. She didn't; and by and by I went again, and then she turned ugly. I looked at her dumfounded when she spoke her real mind and said if we didn't like it we could leave; there were plenty of others. I wouldn't believe my ears even, and said to myself she was worn out with trouble and couldn't mean a word of it. I wanted money for myself, but I wouldn't ask even for anybody but Jenny.

"Next day Madame brought her ten dollars of the two hundred and twenty she owed her, and Jenny got shoes; but it was too late. I knew it well, for I'd seen my sister go the same way. Quick consumption ain't to be stopped with new shoes or anything but new lungs, and there's no patent for them yet that ever I've heard of. She was going last night when I went round, and sure as you live I'm going to put her death in the paper myself. I've been saving my money off lunches to do it, and I'll write it: 'Murdered by a fashionable dressmaker on —— Street, in January, 1886, Jenny G——, age nineteen years and six months.' Maybe they won't put it in, but here it is, ready for any paper that's got feeling enough to care whether sewing-girls are cheated and starved and killed, or whether they get what they've earned. I've got work at home now. It don't matter so much to me; but I'm a committee to attend to this thing, and I'll find out every fraud in New York that I can. I've got nine names now,—three of 'em regular fashionables on the west side, and six of 'em following their example hard as they can on the east; and a friend of mine has printed, in large letters, 'Beware of' at the head of a slip, and I add names as fast as I get them, and every girl that comes in my way I warn against them. Do much good? No. They'll get all the girls they want, and more; but it's some satisfaction to be able to say they are cheats, making a living out of the flesh and blood of their dupes, and I'll say it till I die."

Here stands the experience of one woman with fearlessness enough to protest and energy enough to have at last secured a tolerable living. The report, for such it may be considered, might be made of many more names than those upon her black list, or found on the books of the Union. Happily for the worker, they form but a small proportion of the long list of dressmakers who deal fairly. But the life of the ordinary hand who has not ability enough to rise is, like that of the great majority who depend on the needle, whether machine or hand, filled with hardship, uncertainty, overwork, under-pay. The large establishments have next to no dull season, but we deal in the present chapter only with private workers; and often, on the east side especially, where prices and wages are always at the lowest ebb, the girls who have used all their strength in overwork during the busy season of spring and fall must seek employment in cigar factories or in anything that offers in the intermediate time, the wages giving no margin for savings which might aid in tiding over such periods. The dressmaker herself is often a sufferer, conscienceless customers abounding, who pay for the work of one season only when anxious for that of the next. Often it is mere carelessness,—the recklessness which seems to make up the method of many women where money obligations are concerned; but often also they pass deliberately from one dressmaker to another, knowing that New York holds enough to provide for the lifetime of the most exacting customer. There is small redress for these cases, and the dressmaker probably argues the matter for herself and decides that she has every right, being cheated, to balance the scale by a little of the same order on her own account.

A final form of rascality referred to in a previous chapter is found here, as in every phase of the clothing trade, whether on small or large scale. Girls are advertised for "to learn the trade," and the usual army of applicants appear, those who are selected being told that the first week or two will be without wages, and only the best workers will be kept. Each girl is thus on her mettle, and works beyond her strength and beyond any fair average, to find herself discharged at the end of the time and replaced by an equally eager and equally credulous substitute. There are other methods of fraud that will find place in a consideration of phases of the same work in the great establishments, some difficulties of the employer being reserved for the same occasion.

CHAPTER SIXTH.

MORE METHODS OF PROSPEROUS FIRMS.

TO do justice to employer as well as employed is the avowed object of our search, yet as it goes on, and the methods made necessary by competition become more and more clear, it is evident that back of every individual case of wrong and oppression lies a deeper wrong and a more systematized oppression. Master and servant alike are in the same bonds, and the employer is driven as mercilessly as he drives. He may deny it. He may even be quite unconscious of his own subjection, or, if he thinks at all of its extent, may look enviously at the man or the corporation that has had power to enslave him. The monopolist governs not only the market but the bodies and souls of all who provide wares for that market; yet the fascination of such power is so tremendous that to stand side by side with him is the dream of every young merchant,—the goal on which his eyes are set from the beginning. Only in like power is any satisfaction to be found. Any result below this high-water mark can be counted little else than failure.

To this end, then, toils the employer of every grade, bringing every faculty to bear on the lessening of waste, whether in material or time; the conservation of every force working in line with his purpose. Naturally, the same effect is produced as that mentioned in a previous paper. The employees come to represent "so much producing power," and are driven at full speed or shut off suddenly like the machines of which they are the necessary but still more or less accidental associates. Certain formulas are used, evolved apparently from experience, and carrying with them an assurance of so much grieved but inevitable conviction that it is difficult to penetrate below the surface and realize that, while in degree true, they are in greater degree false. In various establishments, large and small, beginning with one the pay-roll of which carries 1,462 employees, and ending with one having hardly a third this number, the business manager made invariably the same statement: "We make our money from incidentals rather than from any given department. You are asking particularly about suits. I suppose you'll think it incredible, but in suits we work at a dead loss. It is only an accommodation to our customers that makes us keep that department open. The work should be put out to mean any profit, but we can't do that with the choicest materials, and so we make it up in other directions. You would have to go into business yourself to understand just how we are driven."

"Suppose you refused to be driven? A firm of your standing must have matters a good deal in its own hands. Suppose—"

"Suppose!" The manager threw out his hands in a gesture more full of disclaimer than any words. "There is no room for supposes in business, madam. We do what we must. How are we to compete with a factory turning out suits by steam power? Not that we would compete. There is really no occasion," he added hastily. "But their methods certainly have an unpleasant influence, and we are obliged to take them into account slightly."

"Then your statement would be, that no matter how expensive the suit made up, you can make no profit on it?"

"Absolutely none. It is a concession to a customer's whims. We could buy the same thing and sell to her at half the price, but she prefers to select materials and have them put together in our work-room, and we must humor her. But rents are so enormous that the space for every woman employed by us in these departments may be said to represent simply so many cubic feet in good coin, bringing us no return. Our profits are dwindling with every year."

"Might not co-operation—"

Again the manager threw out his hands.

"Simply another form of robbery. We have investigated the history of co-operation, and it does not appear to affiliate with our institutions. The lamentable failure of the Co-operative Dress Association ought to be the answer to that suggestion. No, madam. There is no profit in suits, or in any form of made-up clothing for ladies' wear, if it is done on the premises. You have to turn it over to the wholesale manufacturer if you want profit."

Having heard this statement in many forms, and recognizing the fact that increase in rents as well as in systematized competition might well have reduced profits, it still appeared incredible that the rates charged held no surplus for the firm. Little by little it has become possible to supplement each statement by others of a different order. Nothing is more difficult than to obtain trustworthy information regarding the methods of a firm whose standing is such that to have served it is always a passport to other employment; whose payments are regular, and where every detail of work-room is beyond criticism. It is no question of bare-faced robbery as in that of many cited, yet even here the old story tells itself in different form, and with an element which, in many a less pretentious establishment, has not yet been found to exist.

The work done here is piece-work. French cutters and fitters, receiving from thirty to fifty dollars a week, give that guarantee of style and elegance which is inherent in everything bearing the stamp of the firm. Experts run the machines in the sewing-machine room, being paid by the day at the rate of from six to eight dollars per week in the busy season. The buttonholes are made by women who do nothing else, and who are paid by the dozen, earning from five to seven dollars weekly. All stitched seams are done in the machine-room, and the dress passes from there to the sewing-room, into the hands of the sewing-girls, who receive from three to four dollars and a half for each garment. The latter price is seldom reached; four dollars and a half or five dollars paying for a dress loaded with trimming, puffs, flounces, etc.

At this rate there would seem to be a chance for wages a good deal beyond the average, but it is one of the unwritten laws that no sewing-girl shall exceed five dollars per week; whether formulated by superintendent or by firm remains yet to be discovered. The one unquestionable fact is that if the superintendent of the work-room finds that any girl is expert enough to make over this amount the price per garment is docked, to bring her down to the level. They are never driven. On the contrary, they must wait often, two or three hours at times, for the arrival of "Madame," who must inspect the work, drape a skirt, or give some suggestion as to trimming. No entreaty can induce the superintendent to give out another piece of work which might fill this vacant time, and the girls dare not state their case to the employer. No member of the firm enters the work-rooms. Reports are made by the superintendent of the department, and the firm remains content with knowing that it has provided every comfort for its employees. Complaint would insure discharge, and if a girl hints that she cannot live on five dollars a week the answer has been for the years during which the present superintendent has held the place, always the same:—

"If you haven't a home so that you have no expense of board, it is your own fault, and I can't be expected to do anything about it."

There appears to be no question as to the entire "respectability" of the woman, who would undoubtedly deny the implication contained in her own words. But there is rivalry between the superintendents as to which department shall make largest returns in profits, and wages are kept down to secure that end. There is also no question that a proportion of those employed are "supported," and merely add this work as a means of securing a little more pin-money. It is true of but a very few, but of those few an undeniable fact. It is equally a fact that, in spite of the managers' assertions, profit can be made and is made from this department, and that a large percentage of such profit comes directly from the pocket of the sewing-girl, who, even when she adds buttonhole-making in the simpler dresses, can never pass beyond a fixed wage.

In other large establishments on both sides of the city methods are much the same, with merely slight variations as to comfort of quarters, time for lunch, sanitary conditions, etc. But in all alike, the indispensable, but always very helpless, sewing-girl appears to be one of the chief sources of profit, and to have small capacity and no opportunity for improving her condition. Even where the work comes from the manufactory, and steam has taken the place of foot-power, no machine has yet been run so automatically that the human hand can be entirely dispensed with. The "finisher" remains a necessity, and as finisher sometimes passes slightly beyond the rate obtained when merely sewing-girl. Only slightly, however. It is a deeply rooted conviction among these workers that a tacit or even, it may be, formal understanding has been settled upon by employers in general.

"I don't know how it is," said one of the most intelligent among the many I have talked with; "there's never any trouble about getting work. I've even had them send after me when I had gone somewhere else in hopes of doing better. I used to earn ten and twelve dollars a week on suits, children's or ladies', but now if I earn five or sometimes six I do well. The work goes on with a rush. It's a whole building except the first floor,—five stories, and suits of every kind. The rooms are all crowded, and they give out piece-work, but they've managed it so that we all earn about alike. When the rush of the fall and spring season is over they do white work and flannel skirts and such things, and a great many are discharged in the lull. But go where you will, up-town or down, it doesn't seem to matter how well you can turn off the work or how long you have been at it. They all say, if we ask for better pay, 'It can't be had as long as there is such competition. We're losing straight ahead.' I don't understand. We don't any of us understand, because here is the great rush of work and it must be done. They can't do without us, and yet they are grinding us down so that I get half distracted sometimes, wondering where it will end and if things will ever be better."

"Would not private sewing be better? There is always a demand for good seamstresses."

"I don't know anything about private sewing. You have to cut and plan, and I never learned that. I like to work on things that are cut by a cutter and just so, and I can make up my dozen after dozen with not an eighth of an inch difference in my measurements. I'm an expert, you know."

"But if you learned to do private sewing perfectly you could earn a dollar and a quarter a day and board and have your evening quite free."

The girl shook her head. "I've had that said to me before, but you know it's more independent as I am. Maybe things will be better by and by."

There is no obstinacy like the obstinacy of deep-seated prejudice, and this exists to a bewildering degree among these workers, who, for some inscrutable reason, seem filled with the conviction that private employ of any nature whatever is inevitably a despotism filled with unknown horrors. There appears to be also a certain *esprit du corps* that holds sustaining power. The girl likes to speak of herself as one of such and such a firm's hands, and to regard this distinction as compensation for over-hours and under-pay and all known wretchedness encompassing her trade. The speaker I have quoted was an American girl of twenty-six, had had three years in public schools, and regarded the city as the only place in which life could be considered endurable.

"I shouldn't know what to do in the country if I were there," she said. "I don't seem to like it somehow. It isn't the company, for mother and me keep to ourselves a good deal, but somehow we know how to get along in the city, and the country scares me. I like my work if only I could get more pay for it."

"Do you ever think that if all who work in your line joined together and made common cause you might even things a little; that it might be easier for all of you?"

"We wouldn't dare," she answered, aghast. "Why, do you know, there'd be ten for each one of us that was turned off. Women come there by the hundred. That's what they say to me in our firm: 'What's the use of fussing when here are dozens waiting to take your place?' There isn't any use. They say now that it is the dull season, and they've put our room on flannel skirts; two tucks and a hem, and a muslin yoke that has to be gone round four times with the stitching. One day I made ten, but nine is all one can do without nearly killing themselves, and they pay us one dollar a dozen for making them. It used to be a dollar and a half, and that was fair enough. It's the kind of work I like. I shouldn't be content to do any other; but it's bringing us all down to starvation point, and I think something ought to be done."

In a case like this, and it is the type of many hundreds of skilled workers, who regard their calling with a certain pride, and could by no possibility be induced to seek other lines of work or other methods of living, there seems little to be accomplished. They are, however, but a small portion of the army who wait for some deliverance, and who, if they had been born to a trifle more common sense, would turn in the one sole direction from which relief is certain, this relief and the reasons for and against it having no place at this stage of the investigation.

CHAPTER SEVENTH.

NEGATIVE OR POSITIVE GOSPEL.

FROM the fig-leaf down, it would seem as if a portion of the original curse accompanying it had passed on to each variation or amplification of first methods, its heaviest weight falling always on the weak shoulders that, if endurance could make strong, should belong to-day to a race of giants. Of the ninety and more trades now open to women, thirty-eight involve some phase of this question of clothing, about which centre some of the worst wrongs of modern civilization. It is work that has legitimate place. It must be done by some one, since the exigencies of this same civilization have abolished old methods and made home manufactures seem a poor and most unsatisfactory substitute for the dainty stitching and ornamentation of the cheaper shop-work. It is work that many women love, and, if living wages could be had, would do contentedly from year to year. Of their ignorance and blindness, and the mysterious possession they call pride, and the many stupidities on which their small lives are founded, there is much to be said, when these papers have done their first and most essential work of showing conditions as they are;—as they are, and not as the disciples of *laissez faire* would have us to believe they are.

"It is the business of these philanthropists to raise a hue and cry; to exaggerate every evil and underrate every good. They are not to be trusted. Look at our institutions and see what we are doing for the poor. Study statistics and see how comfortable they are!"

This is the word of a recent correspondent of a Podsnapian turn of mind, who proceeded to present facts and figures bearing out his theory. And on a Sunday shortly after, he was confirmed in his faith and greatly strengthened and comforted by words from a popular preacher, long owner of a popular pulpit, who, standing there as the representative of a master whose message was to the poor, and who turned to them from the beginning, as the hearers who alone could know most truly what meaning the message bore, spoke these words:—

"Moreover, all this hue and cry about so much destitution and misery and the unscrupulous greed of employers is groundless. I am convinced that more than one half—yes, fully three quarters—of the pauperism of which you heard so much in the late campaign exists only in the minds of the Georgeites. The picture drawn of New York's misery is over-colored, and its inspiration is in the distorted imaginations of the George fanatics.... The rum-holes are the cause of all the misery.... I have been watching for thirty-five years, and in all my investigations among the poor I never yet found a family borne down by poverty that did not owe its fall to rum."

This most extraordinary statement, from a man who in one year alone could not have listened to even half the appeals for help likely to have come to him in his position, without discovering that death and disaster in many forms played, if not the chief part, certainly that next in order to rum, can be accounted for only on the ground that a hobby ridden too hard has been known to bear off at the same time both the common-sense and power of judgment of the rider. Prohibition appears to him, as to many another, the only solution; the gospel of negation the only gospel for rich or poor. Since the Church first began to misinterpret the words of its Founder, since men who built hospitals first made the poor to fill them, the "thou shalt not" of the priest has stood in the way of a human development that, if allowed free play, had long ago made its own code, and found in natural spiritual law the key to the overcoming of that formulated by men to whom the divine in man was forever unrecognized and unrecognizable.

This is no place for the discussion of what, to many good men and women, seems the only safety for human kind; but to one who studies the question somewhat at least with the eyes of the physician, it becomes certain that no "thou shalt not" will ever give birth to either conscience or love of goodness and purity and decent living, or any other good that man must know; and that till the Church learns this, her hold on men and women will lessen, year by year. Every fresh institution in the miles of asylums and hospitals that cover the islands of the East River, and stretch on farther and farther with every year, is an added disgrace, an added count in the indictment against modern civilization. There are moments when the student of social conditions abhors Philanthropy; when a disaster that would wipe out at one stroke every institution the city treasures would seem a gift straight from God, if only thereby the scales might fall from men's eyes, and they might learn that hiding foulness in an asylum is not extirpation; that something deeper and stronger than Philanthropy must work, before men can be saved.

It is as student, not as professional philanthropist, that I write; and the years that have brought experience have brought also a conviction, sharpened by every fresh series of facts, that no words, no matter what fire of fervor may lie behind, can make plain the sorrow of the poor. To ears that will hear, to souls that seek forever some way that may help in truth and not in name, even to them it loses power at moments. To souls that sit at ease and leave to "the power that works for righteousness" the evolution of humanity from its prison of poverty and ignorance and pain, it is quite useless to speak. They have their theory, and the present civilization contents them. But for the men and women who are neither Georgeites merely, nor philanthropists merely, nor certain that any sect or creed or ism will help, but who know that the foulest man is still brother, and the wretchedest, weakest woman still sister, whose shame and sorrow not only bear a poison that taints all civilization, but are forever our shame and our sorrow till the world is made clean,—for these men and women I write, not what I fancy, but what I see and know.

Most happily for humanity, they are stronger, more numerous, with every year; but the hardest fact for them remains ever that their battle is a double one, and that, exhausted as they may be with long conflict against lowest forms of evil, they must rally to a sharper one against the army of the Philistines. Strong soul and high endeavor: never since time began has man more needed them; never was there harder work to do.

The story of the working-woman in one great city is, with slight variations in conditions, the story of the working-woman in all; and when we have once settled conclusively what monopoly or competition has done and is doing for New York, we know sufficiently well what Boston and Philadelphia and Chicago and all the host of lesser cities could easily tell us in detail. With the mass of poor who work chiefly to obtain money for drink, and who, with their progeny, are filling the institutions in which we delight, we have absolutely nothing to do. It is seldom from their ranks that workers are recruited. A small proportion, rescued by societies or mission schools, may be numbered among them, but the greater part are a grade above, and while perhaps wellnigh as ignorant, have an inheritance of better instincts, and could under any reasonable conditions of living find their fate by no means intolerable.

I have chosen to-day, instead of passing on to another form of the clothing trade, to return to that of underwear, and this because it is the record most crowded with cases in which the subjects could not enter household service and have not been reduced to poverty by intemperance. Nor is the selection made with a view to working up as startling a case as possible. On the contrary, it has been made almost at random from the many recorded, any separate mention of which would be impossible in the space at command. First on the long list comes Catherine E——, an "expert" in underwear, and living on the top floor of a large, old-fashioned house in Clinton Place; the lower part stores and offices, the upper a tenement. She earned three years ago $1.50 a day; at times, $1.75. The same work now brings her eighty-five cents, and now and then but seventy-five. The husband was a "boss painter," and they were comfortable, even prosperous, till the fate of his calling came upon him, and first the "drop hand," and later blood-poisoning and heart-disease followed. He is just enough alive to care a little for the children and to oversee the pitiful household affairs; the oldest girl, a child of seven, doing the marketing, boiling the kettle, etc., and this season going to school. They are fair-faced, gentle children, and this is their mother's story:—

"I can run the machine, and I did with every one of them when they were two weeks old, for I've always been strong. Nothing that happens is bad enough to kill me, and it's lucky it's so, for it's two years and over since William there could earn a dollar. He helps me; but you see for yourself he's half dead and no getting well, because we've nothing to buy food with, or medicine, or anything that could help him. We were both brought up here in the city. We don't know anything about the country, but sometimes I wish we did, and that I could take the children and live somehow. But I don't know how people live there. I'm certain of work here, and I'd be afraid to go anywhere else. I'm making babies' slips now; three tucks and a hem and find your own cotton, and it takes eighteen hours to make a dozen, and these are seventy-five cents a dozen. I can buy cotton at eighteen cents a dozen, but we have to take it from the manufacturer at twenty cents—sometimes twenty-five cents. Last week I was on corset-covers; I take whatever they send up, for I'm an old hand, and always sure of work. They were plain corset-covers, and I got forty cents a dozen without the buttonholes. If I did them it would be five cents on every dozen, and sometimes I do. That pile in the corner is extra-size chemises. I get $1.50 a dozen for making them, and if I cord the bands, fifty cents a dozen for them. I can do seven or eight a day; but there are no more just now, they say. I work fourteen hours a day; yes, I've often worked sixteen, for you see there are six of us, and we must be clothed and fed. William is handy, but, poor soul! he's only a man, and he's sick past cure, and nobody but me for us all. God help us! I wouldn't mind if wages were steady, but they cut and cut, and always some excuse for making them lower, and here am I, that can do anything, private orders and all, down to eighty-five cents a day. I could earn more by family sewing, but I can't leave William or the children, for he's likely to go any minute, the doctors say, if he over-exerts himself; and suppose it came, and I not here, and the baby and Willie and all! I've turned all ways. I think and think as I sit here, and there's no help in God or man. It's all wrong somehow, but we don't know why nor how, and the only way I can see is just to die. There's no place for honesty or hard work. You must lie and cheat if you want standing room. God help us!—if there is a God; but I've my doubts. Why don't he help, if there is one?"

Here the average earnings were twenty-five dollars a month, the rent of the room they occupied seven dollars, leaving eighteen dollars for food, fire, light, and clothing.

Another disabled husband, recovering, but for many months unable to work, was found in a tenement-house in East Eleventh Street. In this case work and earnings were almost identical with the last, but there were but two children, and thus less demand for food, etc. For a year and a half the wife, though also an "expert," had never exceeded eighty-five cents a day and had sometimes fallen as low as seventy. She had sometimes gone to the factory instead of working at home, and the last firm employing her in this way had charged ten cents on the dollar for the steam used in running the machine which she operated.

"It didn't pay," the little woman said, with a laugh that ended as a sob, checked instantly. "I could earn eight dollars a week, but there was the steam, ten cents on the dollar, and my car fares, for there was no time to walk,—sixty cents for them,—$1.40, you see, altogether. I might as well work at home and have the comfort of seeing that the children were all right. There's plenty of work, it seems. It's wages that's the trouble, and do you know how they cut them? If I could work any other way I would, but I like to sew, and I don't know any other trade. I'm not strong, but somehow I can run the machines, and there's nothing else. But we're clean discouraged. It isn't living, and we don't know what way to turn."

In East Sixth Street, near the Bowery, Mrs. W., a widow still young and with a nervously energetic face and manner, gave her experience. She had been forewoman in a factory before her husband's death, having supported him through his last year of life, working all day and nursing him at night. In this way her own health broke down, and she was at last taken to the hospital, where she remained nearly six months, coming out to find her place filled, but a subordinate one open to her.

"I had to wait for that," she said, "and I had to learn. I knew a sewing-machine place where often you could get ruffling for skirts to do, and I went up there one morning. It was the three tucks and a hem ruffling, and I did one hundred and forty-two yards from eight in the morning till half-past four, and they paid me twenty-three cents. 'We could get it done for that by steam power,' they said, 'so we can't give more. It's a favor anyway to give it out at all.' That was my first day's work. The next I went down to my place on Canal Street. They think a good deal of me there, and they put me on drawers right away; thirty-five cents a dozen for making them. I can make two dozen a day sometimes, but fine ones not over a dozen, though they pay fifty cents. You wonder how they make anything. I've been forewoman, and I know the prices. Why, even at forty cents a pair they make on them. Twenty-one yards of cloth at five cents makes a dozen; that's $1.05; and eighteen yards of edge at four and a half cents, that's eighty-one cents; and the making thirty-five cents; that's $2.21. Thread and all, they won't cost over $2.25, and they sell at wholesale at three dollars a dozen and retail at $4.80. There's profit even when you think a cent couldn't be made. Take skirts, three yards of cloth in each at six cents. They pay thirty cents a dozen for tucking, twenty-five cents a dozen for ruffling, and thirty cents for seaming,—eighty-five cents a dozen for the entire skirt; and the cloth makes it, at eighteen cents apiece, $3.01 for the dozen. Those skirts retail at sixty cents apiece, and wholesale at fifty cents. There's profit on them all, no matter what they say, for I've figured every penny over and over, down to the tape and thread. But they swear to you they are ruined by competition, and so the wages go down and down and down. Leave the city? I don't know how to live anywhere else. I've never learned. It's something to be sure of your work, even if it is starvation wages. But there's distress all around me. I don't see what it means. There's a girl in the room next to me, with an invalid mother. She does flannel shirts, but before she got them she nearly starved on underwear. Now she earns a dollar a day, but she works fourteen hours for it, seven cents an hour. That's nice pay in a Christian land. Christian! Bah! I used to believe there was Christianity, but I've given it up, like many another. There's just one religion left, and that is the worship of money. The Golden Calf is God, and every man sells his soul for a chance to bow to it. I don't know but what I would myself. So far I've kept decent; I came of decent folks; but it's no fault of many a man that I've worked for that I can say so still. I've had to leave three places because they wouldn't let me alone, and I stay where I am now because they're quiet, respectable people, and no outrageousness. But if you know what it all means I wish you'd tell me, for I'm dazed, and I can't make out the reason of anything any more."

In the same house a widow with three children,—the father killed by falling from a scaffolding,—earns sixty cents a day by making buttonholes, and above her is another well past sixty, whose trade and wages are the same. How they live, what they can wear, how they are fed, on this amount is yet to be told, but every detail waits; and having gathered them from these and other women in like case, I am not yet prepared to believe that they live at ease, or that the "hue and cry about so much destitution and misery, and the unscrupulous greed of employers, is groundless."

CHAPTER EIGHTH.

THE TRUE STORY OF LOTTE BAUER.

IT was the Prussian War that seemed to settle the question. So far as Grossvater Bauer himself was concerned, he would still have toiled on contentedly. To be alive at all on German soil was more than honor or wealth or any good thing that the emigrant might report as part of his possession in that America to which all discontented eyes looked longingly. The reports might all be true; yet why should one for the sake of better food or more money be banished from the Vaterland and have only a President, a man of the people, in place of the old Kaiser, whose very name thrilled the heart, and for whose glory Grossvater Bauer would have given many sons? He had given them. Peace had come, and France was paying tribute; and, one by one, the few who had escaped French bullets came home to the little Prussian village and told their tales of the siege and of the three who had fallen at Sedan. Grossvater Bauer sat silent. He had been as silent when they brought the news to him in the beginning. It was the fortune of war. He had served his own time, and having served it, accepted as part of his birthright the same necessity for his sons. They had worked side by side with him on the great farm where he had been for most of his life head laborer and almost master; worked contentedly until Annchen, the oldest daughter, had married a tailor, dissatisfied like all tailors, and set sail for the strange country where fortune had always open hands for all the world. He had prospered, and in Annchen's letters, coming at rare intervals, was always an appeal to them to come over. The boys listened; doubtfully at first, for the father's faith was strong in them that no land could ever hold the same good as this land through which the Rhine flowed to the sea. But as the time came when they must enter the army there was rebellion. Here and there, in the air it seemed, for no one could say from whence the new feeling had come, were questions the sound of which was not to be tolerated by any true Prussian. Why should this great army live on the toil of the peasant? Why should the maintenance of these conscripts swallow up every possible saving in the wages and be the largest item save one in the year's expenses? Why should there be a standing army at all?

Hans, when his time came, had learned to ask, but he had not learned to answer. The splendor of his uniform appeared to be in some sort a reply, and its tightness may also have had its effect in restricting his mental operations. For three years the carefully kept accounts of Grossvater Bauer held the item: "Maintenance of son in army, $121.37." Then Hans came home and married Lieschen, the little dairy-maid, and in due time Lotte's blue eyes opened on the world whose mysteries were still not quite explicable to the heavy father. Wilhelm and Franz had taken their turn, and in spite of questions settled passively at last into the farm life. Then came the war,—the war that called for every man with strength to carry a gun,—and when it was over Lotte was fatherless, and there were no more sons to bear the name, or to trouble Grossvater Bauer's mind with further questions.

Very glorious, but what use if there were no boys left to whom the story could be told? If he had yielded, if even one had crossed the sea, there would be something still to live for. But Lieschen had given them no boys. He thought of it day after day, till the familiar fields grew hateful and he wished only to escape from the land to which he had paid a tax too heavy for mortal endurance. There was no one but Lieschen and her little ones, Lotte first of all and best beloved, and in another month they had set sail and the old life was over.

"Work for all, homes for all, plenty for all," Annchen had written how many times. Yet now, when the Grossvater appeared, and the round-eyed Lieschen and her tribe of five, Peter shook his head. He had prospered, it is true. From journeyman tailor he had become master on a small scale, and packed himself and his men into a shop so tiny that it was miraculous how elbow-room remained to use the goose. But work for the Grossvater was quite another thing. He had no trade, and while his capacity as farmer on scientific methods ought to give him paying employment in the country, the city held nothing for him. Work for Lieschen and Lotte was easy. A week or two of apprenticeship would teach them all that need be known to do the work on cheap coats or pantaloons, but even for them it was certain that the country would be better.

It was here that Grossvater Bauer developed unexpected obstinacy. He had a little money. He was still strong and in good case. Here was this great city which must have work of some nature, and which, so far from weighing upon him as Lotte had feared, seemed to have for him a curious fascination. He haunted the wharves. The smell of the sea and the tarred ropes of the ships bewitched him, and on the wharves he soon found work, and loaded and unloaded all day contentedly, with a feeling that this was after all more like living than anything could have been in the home fields where only the ghosts of his own remained to have place at his side.

It is now only that the story of Lotte begins,—Lotte, who pined for the great farm and the fields across which the wind swept, and the cows she had named and cared for. Her mother forgot, or did not care. She had never loved her work, and liked better to chatter with the other women in the house, or even to run the machine hour after hour, than to milk, or feed the cattle, or churn. Lotte hated the machine. Her back ached, her eyes burned, and her head throbbed after only an hour or two of it. "Let me take a place," she begged, but the Grossvater shook his head angrily. This was a free country. There was no need that she should serve. Let her learn to be contented and thankful that she could earn so much. For with their simple habits the wages paid in 1881 seemed wealth. Forty-five cents a pair, three of which she could make in a day, brought the week's earnings to eight dollars, sometimes to nine dollars, and Peter prophesied that it might even be ten or twelve dollars. Lieschen had as much. Down on the wharves the Grossvater earned sometimes eighteen dollars a week. It was a fortune. At home, in the best of times, with sons and daughters all at work, his books, which he kept always with the accuracy of a merchant, showed something under $1,000 a year as receipts, the expenses hardly varying from the $736.28 which represented the maintenance of the family during Hans's first year as soldier. Their food ration at home had been nine and a half cents daily. Wheat bread had stood for festivals and high days. Black bread, cabbage soup, beer, cheese, and sausage, with meat on Sundays, had been their only ambition as to food, and here Grossvater Bauer insisted upon the same regimen, and frowned as one by one the fashions of the new country crept in. Peter had been right after all. One must work, it is true, but no harder and no longer, and the return was double. The little iron chest which had held the savings at home held them here, and at rare intervals the Grossvater allowed Lotte to look, and said as he turned over the shining coins, "Thou wilt have most, my Lottchen. It is for thee that I put them away."

"There is enough for a little farm," Lotte said one day. "We could go on this Long Island and have land, and not be shut all day in these dark rooms."

"That is slower," the Grossvater said. "We will go back with much money when it is earned, and I shall be owner, and thou, Lotte, the mistress, and Franz maybe will go also."

Lotte shook her head, though her cheeks were pink.

"Franz cares only for America," she said. "Come with us some day, Grossvater, and let us look at the little house he knows. There is land, two acres, and a barn and a cow, and all for so little. I could be stronger then."

"That is folly," the old man said angrily. "It would be but shillings there, where here it is dollars. Wait and you will see."

Lotte looked after him wonderingly as he turned away. To save was becoming his passion. He grudged her even her shoes and the dress she must have, though no one had so little. Peter revolted openly and came less and less. Lieschen cried, but still looked at the week's wages as compensation for many evils, and Lotte worked on, the pink spot fixing itself on her cheeks, and her blue eyes growing sadder with every week. Franz, the son of their old neighbor at home, hated this crowded city as she did, and urged her to take her chances and marry him, even if, as yet, he was only laborer in the market gardens out on the Island. There were minutes when Lotte nearly yielded, but the Grossvater seemed to hold her as with chains. She loved him, and she had always submitted. Perhaps in time he would yield and learn again to care for the old life of the country.

At last a change came, but there was in it no release, only closer imprisonment. Peter and Annchen had followed a brother to Chicago and opened a shop double the size of the old one, and they were hardly settled when Lieschen sickened suddenly and after long illness died. For many weeks there was no earning. Even the angry Grossvater saw that it was impossible, and doled out reluctantly the money they had helped him to save. Lieschen had always fretted him. Lotte was the best gift she had ever made the Bauer name, and when the funeral was over, he went home, secretly relieved that the long watch was over; went home to find that the precious chest, hidden always under piles of bedding in the closet where he locked his own possessions, had disappeared. There had been a moving from the story above. Men had gone up and down for an hour, and no one had noticed specially what was carried. There was no clew, even after days of searching; and Grossvater Bauer, who had rushed madly to the police station, haunted it now, with imploring questions, till told they could do nothing and that he must keep away. He sank then into the sort of apathy that had held him when the news came from Sedan. He went to his work, but there was no heart in it, and sat by the fire when night came, with only an impatient shake of the head when Lotte tried to comfort him. Till then no one had realized his age, but now his hair whitened and his broad shoulders bowed. He was an old man; and Lotte said to herself that his earning days were nearly over, and worked an hour or two later that the week's gain might be a little larger and so comfort him.

She came home one afternoon with her bundle of work. Gretchen, who was nearly thirteen, had helped her carry it, and had shrunk back frightened as the foreman put a finger under her chin, and nodded smilingly at the peach-like face and the great blue eyes. Lotte struck down his hand passionately. She knew better than Gretchen what the smile meant. The child should never know if she could help it, and she did not mind the evil glance that followed her toward the door. There were people standing at their doors as she went slowly up the stairs, her breath coming quickly, as now it always did when she climbed them.

"Poor soul!" one of them said. "She little knows what she's coming to."

"Was ist los?" Lotte cried as the door opened, and then shrieked aloud, for the Grossvater lay there on the bed, crushed and disfigured and almost speechless, but lifting one hand feebly as she flew toward him.

"A sugar hogshead," somebody said. "It rolled over him when he thought it was firm, and brought down some barrels with it. He's past helping. May the saints have a heart for the poor children! He would be brought here, but what will you do with him?"

"There'll be naught to do by morning," said another. "Can't you see he's going?" But by morning no change had come, nor for many mornings. The wounds and bruises slowly healed, but save for the one hand that moved toward her, there were no signs of life. The strong body held by paralysis might linger for years, and Lotte must earn for him and for all. Even then a living might have been possible, for Gretchen had a place as cash-girl and earned two dollars a week, and Lisa was promised one after New Year's. But it was a hard winter. They ate only what they must, and Lotte's blue eyes looked out from hollow sockets, and she shivered with cold. Wages had fallen, and they fell faster and faster till by January her ten and twelve hours' work brought her but six dollars instead of the eight or nine she had always earned. The foreman she hated made everything as difficult as possible. Though the bundle came ready from the cutting room, he had managed more than once to slip out some essential piece, and thus lessened her week's wages, no price being paid where a garment was returned unfinished. He had often done this where girls had refused his advances, yet it was impossible to make complaint. The great house on Canal Street left these matters entirely with him, and regarded complaint as mere blackmailing. Lotte tried others, but wages were even less. She was sure of work here, and pay was prompt. With the spring things must be better. But long before the spring Lisa had sickened and died, and Lotte buried her in the Potter's Field, and hurried home to make up the lost time, and hush the crying little ones as she could. It did not occur to her that she could write to Annchen and ask for help, and Franz had quarrelled with her because she did not put the Grossvater in a hospital and send the children to some asylum.

"I will even marry you with the children," he said, "but never with the Grossvater who hindered and spoiled everything."

"He has cared for me always, even when he was hard," said Lotte. "I shall care for him now;" and Franz rushed away and had come no more.

For a year Lotte's struggle went on. She knew only the one form of work; and she dared not take time to learn another.

"If it were not for the Grossvater," she said, "and the children, I should have a place and work in the country and grow strong, but I cannot. If I die before them what can they do?"

There was other trouble. Gretchen's light little head could never guard her pretty face. She was fourteen now, and tall and fair, fretting against the narrow life and refusing to stay indoors when evening came. One day she did not come home; and when Lotte sought her she saw only the evil smile and triumphant eyes of the foreman who had followed her a year ago and who laughed in her face as he shut the door.

"You'd better come in yourself," he called. "You'd fare better if you did."

Lotte went home dumb, and sat down at her machine. There was no money in the house, nor would be till she had taken home this work; but as she bent over it the blood poured in a stream from her mouth. She tried to rise, but fell back; and when the screaming children had brought in neighbors, Lotte's struggle was quite over. When they had buried her in the Potter's Field by Lisa, they took the bundle of work stained with her life-blood and carried it back to its owners.

"She'll need no more," said the old neighbor from the floor above as she laid it on the counter. "You've cut her down and cut her down, till there wasn't life left to stand it longer. There's not one of you to blame, you say, but I that know, know you've fastened her coffin-lid with nails o' your own makin', an' that sooner or later you'll come face to face, an' find that red-hot is cowld to the hate that's makin' ready for you. An' as for him that stands there smilin', if it weren't for the laws that spare the guilty and send the innocent to their deaths, God knows it would be the best thing these hands ever did to tear him to bits. But there's no one to blame. Ye're sure o' that. Wait a while. The day's comin' when you'll maybe think different; an' may God speed it!"

CHAPTER NINTH.

THE EVOLUTION OF A JACKET.

"IF underwear, whether for men or women, has proven itself a most excellent medium for starvation; if suits and dresses in general rank but a grade above; if shirts, whether of cotton or woollen, are a despair; and in each and all competition has cheapened material and manufacture and brought labor to the 'life limit' and below, at least it cannot be so bad with cloaks and jackets. Here are single garments, often of the most expensive material and put together in the most finished and perfect manner. Skilled labor is demanded, careful handling, spotless neatness. Here is one industry which must give not only a living wage, but a surplus. These women must be on the way to at least semi-prosperity."

This was the thought in the days in which one phase after another of the underwear problem presented itself, each one more bewildering, more heart-sickening, than the last. Here and there had been the encounter with one who had always been sure of work and who had never failed to receive a fair return. But the summary had been inevitably as it stands recorded,— overwork, under-pay; a fruitless struggle against overwhelming odds.

With this thought the quest began anew. The manufacturers of cloaks and jackets reported "piece-work" as the rule. The great dry-goods establishments had the same word. Here and there was one where work was done on the premises, and where skilled hands held the same places year after year, the wages ranging from six to ten dollars, hardly varying. But for most of them the same causes stated in the third chapter, "The Methods of a Prosperous Firm," have operated, and it has been found expedient to settle upon "piece-work" and let rent be paid and space be furnished by the workers themselves.

"They like it better," said the business manager of the great firm against whom there have never been charges of dishonesty or unkindness in their treatment of employees. "It would be impossible to do all our work on the premises. We should want the entire block if we even half did it. But we know some of the women, and we pay as high as anybody; perhaps higher. It saves them car fares and going out in all weathers, and a great many other inconveniences, when they work at home, and I don't see why there should be any objections made. The amount of it is, there are too many women. The best thing to be done is to ship them West. They say they're wanted there, and there is certainly not room enough for them here. Machinery will soon take their place, anyway. I have one in mind now that ought to do the work of ten women perfectly, and require simply a tender and finisher. We shall get the thing down to a fine point very soon. Hard on the women? Why, no. We always hold on to first-class workers, and there's nothing much to be done with second and third class except to use them through the busy season, and let them go in the dull."

"Go where?"

The manager paused and looked reflectively at his well-kept finger-nails.

"My dear madam, that's a question I have no time to consider. I dare say they earn a living somehow. Indeed, I'm told they go into cigar factories. There's always plenty of work."

"Plenty of work,"—a form of words so familiar that I looked for it now from both employer and employed. But for the last was an addition finding no place on the lips of the first: "Plenty of work? Oh, yes! I can always get plenty of work. The trouble is to get the wages for it."

A block or so below, and further west, one great window of a cheaper establishment held jackets and wraps large and small, marked down for the holidays, their advertisement in a morning paper having read, "Jackets from $4 up." Still further over, another window displayed numbers as great, and a placard at one side announced: "These elegant jackets from $2.87 up." The cloth might be shoddy, but here was a garment, fashionably cut, well finished to all appearance, and unexceptionable in pattern and color. All along the crowded avenue the story was the same, and as east took the place of west, and Grand Street and the Bowery and Third Avenue gave in their returns, "These elegant jackets from $2.35 up" gave the final depth to which cheapness could descend.

If this was retail, what could be the wholesale price, and what was likely to be the story of the worker from whose hands they had come? It is worth while to follow these jackets as they emerge from the cutting-room, and in packages holding such number of dozens as has been agreed upon, pass to the express wagon which distributes them among the workers, the firm in mind at present, like many others, preferring this arrangement to any which involves dealing directly with the women.

First on the list stands the name of a woman a little over fifty years old, whose husband is a painter and who left Germany eight years ago, urged to come over by a daughter more adventurous than the rest, who had married and emigrated at once. Work was plentiful when they arrived, and the husband found immediate employment at his trade, with wages so high that the wife had no occasion for any employment outside her own rooms. The youngest child, a girl of nine, went to school. They lived in comfortable rooms on a decent street, put money in a savings bank, and felt that America held more good even than the name had always seemed to promise. Then came the financial troubles of 1879 and 1881, the gradual fall of wages, the long seasons when there was no work, and last, the fate that overtakes the worker in lead, whether painter or in any other branch,—first painter's colic, and the long train of symptoms preceding the paralysis which came at last, the stroke a light one, but leaving the patient with the "drop hand" and all the other complications, testifying that the working days were over. Strength enough returned for an odd job now and then, and the little man accepted his fate cheerily, and congratulated himself that the bank held a little fund and that thus the lowering wages could be pieced out. The bank settled this question by almost immediate failure; a long and expensive illness for the wife followed; and when it ended furniture and small valuables of every sort had been pawned, and they left the empty rooms for narrower quarters and sought for work in which all could share. To add to the complication, the daughter, who had had good sense enough to take a place as child's nurse, broke her leg, and became, even when able to walk again, too disabled to return to this work. She could run the machine, and her mother was an expert buttonhole-maker and had already learned various forms of work on cloth, both in cheap coats and pantaloons, and in jackets and cloaks. The jackets seemed to promise most, for in 1884 each one brought to the maker sixty cents, buttonholes being $1.50 per hundred, the presser receiving ten cents each and the finisher six cents, these amounts being deducted from the price paid on each. To save this amount the husband learned how to press, and though his crippled hands can barely grasp the iron, and often his wife must help him place the cramped fingers in position, he stands there smiling and well content to add this mite to the fund. For a year their home has been in a deep basement, where, save at noonday, it is impossible to run the machines without artificial light. A dark room opens from the one in which they work, itself dark, unventilated save from the hall, and chosen as abiding place because it represents but four dollars a month in rent. Two machines run by mother and daughter stand as near the window as possible, and close by is the press-board and the pale but optimistic little man, who looks proudly at each seam as he lays it open. Jackets are everywhere,—piled on chairs and scattered over the floor,—waiting the various operations necessary before they can at last be bundled on the ex-painter's back, who smiles to himself as he toils down to the firm's headquarters, reflecting that he has saved the expressage another week. What are the returns? Lisa will give them,—the wife whose English is still uncertain, and whose gentle, anxious eyes grow eager and bright as she talks, the husband nodding confirmation, or shaking his head as he sees the tears come suddenly, with a "Not so, not so, Lisa."

"I know not if we shall live at all," she says. "For see. We two, my Gretchen and I, we make but ten for a day. Tree dollar? Yes, but you must take from it de buttonhole an' finish and much else, and it is so short—so short that we can work on them. The season, that is it—six weeks—two months, maybe, and then pantaloon till spring jacket come. See. It is early that we begin,—seven, maybe,—and all day we shall sew and sew. We eat no warm essen. On table dere is bread and beer in pitcher and cheese to-day. We sit not down, for time goes away so. No, we stand and eat as we must, and sew more and more. Ten jackets to one day—so Gretchen and me can make ten jackets to one day, but we sit always—we go not out. It is fourteen hours efery day—yes, many time sixteen—we work and work. Then we fall on bed and sleep, and when we wake again it is work always. And I must stop a leetle; not much, but a leetle, for my back have such pain that I fall on the bed to say, 'Ach Gott! is it living to work so in this rich, free America?' But he is sick always, my man, even if he will laugh. He say he must laugh alway for two because I cannot. For when this work is past it is only pantaloons, and sew so hard as we may it is five, six pair maybe, for Gretchen and me all day, and that not always. Many day we do nothing because they say work is dull, and then goes away all we save before. But we need not to ask help. So much is good that we work and earn, but I think I die soon of my pain, and who then helps his fingers so stiff to press or thinks how he will ache even when he will laugh? It is because America is best that we come, but how is it best to die because it is always work and no joy, no hope, never one so small stop?"

"Never one so small stop." The attic had the same story, and the white-faced, hollow-eyed woman who tried to smile as she spoke turned also from the waiting pile of jackets and drew one or two back to the sheet spread for them on the floor to which they had slipped. A table and two chairs, a small stove in which burned bare handful of coals, the two machines, at one of which a girl of twenty still sewed on, and in the corner a bed, on which lay another girl of the same age, but with the crimson spot on her cheeks and the shining eyes of advanced consumption. It had been one of the faces so often seen behind the counters of the great stores, delicate in features and coloring, with soft dark eyes and fair masses of hair loose on the pillow.

"I try to keep her tidy," the mother said, "but she can't bear her hair up a minute, it's so heavy on her head, an' I've no time to 'tend to it but the minute I take in the morning. It's jackets now that I'm on. I thought maybe there'd be less risk in them than cloaks. Cloaks seem to give 'em so much chance to cheat. I wouldn't work at all at home, I'd be out doing by the day, for I had a good run of work, but there's Maggie, and I can't leave her, though God knows she gets little good of me but the knowing I'm here. I'll tell you what they did to me on cloaks. I work for S—— & Co., far down on Broadway, and they give out the most expensive kind of cloaks, and nine dollars a dozen for the making; other kinds, too, but I'd been on them a good while and knew just how. The pay was regular, but before I'd had work from them a month I saw they were bound to make complaints and dock pay whether there was any fault in the work or not. One and another took their turn, and no help for it; for if they complained the foreman just said: 'You needn't take any work unless you like. There are plenty waiting to fill your place.' Poor souls! What could they do but go on?

"At last came my turn. He tossed them all over. 'It's poor work,' he said. 'They're not finished properly. You can't be paid for botching. There's three dollars, and that's too much.' 'The work is the same it's always been. There's no botching,' I said; but he held out the three dollars. 'No,' I said, 'If you won't pay fair I'll go to the Woman's Protective Union and see what they'll do.' His face was black as thunder. 'Take your money,' he says, holding out the rest, 'but you may sing for more work from this establishment,' and he flung the money on the floor. That didn't trouble me, because I knew I could get work just below, and I did that same day; twenty cloaks, ten to be made at sixty cents apiece, and ten at fifty-five cents. I had Angie here to help, and when they were done I carried them down. This man was a Jew, but there's small difference. If the Jew knew best how to cheat in the beginning, the Christian caught up with him long ago. 'The buttons are all on wrong,' he said. 'I told you to set them an inch further back. We'll have to alter them every one and charge you for the time.' 'I can take oath they are on as I was told to put them on,' I said, 'but if they must be changed I'll change them myself and save the money.'

"It took long talking to make him agree, but at last he said I could come next morning but one, and he'd let me alter them as a great favor. I did come down, but he said they couldn't wait and had made the change, and he charged me six dollars for what he said was my mistake. It was no use to complain. He could swear I had done the job wrong, and so I went home with $5.50 instead of eleven dollars for nearly a fortnight's work. I changed the place, and so far nobody has docked me; but doing my best, and Angie working as steady as I do, we can't make more than twenty cents on a jacket, and it's a short season. When it's over I do coats, but it's less pay than jackets, and there's living and Maggie's medicine and the doctor, though he won't take anything. I'd feel better if he did, but he won't. Angie used to be in a factory, but there's the baby now, and she doesn't know what way to turn but this. See, he's here by Maggie." The sick girl lifted a corner of the quilt, and something stirred,—a baby of seven or eight months whose great eyes looked out from a face weazened and sharpened, deep experience seeming graven in every line.

"He's a wise one," the sick girl said. "He's found it's no use to cry, and he likes to be by me because it's warm. But he frightens me sometimes, for he just lies and looks at me as if he knew a million things and could tell them every one. He's always hungry, and maybe that makes him wiser. I'm sure I could tell some things that people don't know."

The words came with gasps between. It was plain that what she had to tell must find speedy listener if it were to be heard at all, but for that day at least the story must wait. Here, as in other places, the cloakmaker was earning from sixty to seventy cents a day, but even this was comfort and profusion compared with the facts that waited in a Fourth Ward street, and in a rookery not yet reached by any sanitary laws the city may count as in operation. Here and there still remains one of the old wooden houses with dormer windows, a remnant of the city's early days and given over to the lowest uses,—a saloon below and tenements above. In one of these, in a room ten feet square, low-ceiled, and lighted by but one window whose panes were crusted with the dirt of a generation, seven women sat at work. Three machines were the principal furniture. A small stove burned fiercely, the close smell of red-hot iron hardly dominating the fouler one of sinks and reeking sewer-gas. Piles of cloaks were on the floor, and the women, white and wan, with cavernous eyes and hands more akin to a skeleton's than to flesh and blood, bent over the garments that would pass from this loathsome place saturated with the invisible filth furnished as air. They were handsome cloaks, lined with quilted silk or satin, trimmed with fur or sealskin, and retailing at prices from thirty to seventy-five dollars. A teapot stood at the back of the stove; some cups and a loaf of bread, with a lump of streaky butter, were on a small table absorbing their portion also of filth. An inner room, a mere closet, dark and even fouler than the outer one, held the bed; a mattress, black with age, lying on the floor. Here such as might be had was taken when the sixteen hours of work ended,—sixteen hours of toil unrelieved by one gleam of hope or cheer; the net result of this accumulated and ever-accumulating misery being $3.50 a week. Two women, using their utmost diligence, could finish one cloak per day, receiving from the "sweater," through whose hands all must come, fifty cents each for a toil unequalled by any form of labor under the sun, unless it be that of the haggard wretches dressed in men's clothes, but counted as female laborers, in Belgian mines. They cannot stop, they dare not stop, to think of other methods of earning. They have no clothing in which they could obtain even entrance to an intelligence office. They have no knowledge that could make them servants of even the meanest order. They are what is left of untrained, hopelessly ignorant lives, clinging to these lives with a tenacity hardly higher in intelligence than that of the limpet on the rock, but turning to one with lustreless eyes and blank faces, holding only the one question,—"Lord, how long?" They are one product of nineteenth-century civilization, and these seven are but types, hundreds of their kind confronting the searcher, who looks on aghast and who, as the list lengthens and case after case gives in its unutterably miserable details, turns away in a despair only matched by that of the worker. Yet they are here, this army of incompetents, marching through torture to their graves; and till we have found some method by which torture may lessen, these lives as they vanish pass on to the army of avengers, and will face us by and by when excuses fall away and Justice comes face to face with the weak souls that failed in the flesh to know its nature or its demand.

CHAPTER TENTH.

BETWEEN THE RIVERS.

"THE nearer the river the nearer to hell."

It was a strong word, and the big chest from which it issued held more of the same sort,—a tall worker, carpenter apparently, hurrying on with his box of tools and talking, as he went, with a companion half his size, but with quite his power of expression, interjecting strange German oaths as he listened to the story poured out to him. With that story we have at present nothing to do. But the first words lingered, and they linger still as the summary of such life as is lived by many workers on east and west sides alike.

Were the laws governing a volume of this nature rigidly observed, the present phase of this investigation could hardly be the point at which to stop for any detail of how these workers live from day to day. But as the search has gone on through these hours when Christmas joy is in the air, when the smallest shop hangs out its Christmas token, and the great stores are thronged with buyers far into the evening, I think of the lives in which Christmas has no place, of the women for whom all days are alike, each one the synonyme of relentless, unending toil; of the children who have never known a childhood and for whom Christmas is but a name. For even when mission and refuge have done their utmost, there is still the army unreached by any effort and in great part unreachable, no method recorded in any system of the day having power to drag them to the light and thus make known to us what manner of creature it is that cowers in shadowy places and has no foothold in the path we call progress. That their own ignorance holds them in these shadows, bound as with chains; that even a little more knowledge would break the bonds, in part at least, has no present bearing on the fact that thousands are alive among us to whom existence has brought only pain, and that fresh thousands join this dumb throng of martyrs with every added year. If they had learned in any degree how to use to the best advantage the pittance earned, there would be less need of these chapters; yet as I read the assurances of our political economists, that a wage of four dollars per week is sufficient, if intelligently used, to supply all the actual necessities of the worker, the question pushes itself between the lines: "Why should they be forced to know only necessities; and is this statement made of any save those too ignorant to define their wants and needs, too helpless to dare any protestation, even if more knowledge had come?"

The professional political economist of the old school, the school to which all but a handful belong, takes refuge in the census returns as the one reply to any arraignment of the present. Blind as a bat to any figures save his own, he answers all complaint with the formula: "In 1860 the property of this country, equally divided, would have given every man, woman, and child $514 each. In 1870 the share would have been $624; in 1880, $814. In 1886 returns are not in, but $900 and more would be the division per capita. What madness to talk of suffering when this flood of wealth pours through the land. Admitting that the lowest class suffer, it is chiefly crime, drunkenness, etc., that bring suffering. The majority are perfectly comfortable."

Having read this statement in many letters and heard it in interviews as well, it seems plain that the conviction embodied in both has fastened itself upon that portion of the public whose thinking is done for them, and who range themselves by choice with that order who would not be convinced "even though one rose from the dead." "The majority are perfectly comfortable." Let us see how comfortable.

I turn first to the pair, a mother and daughter, a portion of whose experience found place in the chapter on "More Methods of Prosperous Firms." Here, as in so many cases, there had been better days, and when these suddenly ended a period of bewildered helplessness, in which the widow felt that respectability like hers must know no compromise, and that any step that would involve her "being talked about" was a step toward destruction. She must live on a decent street, in a house where she need not be ashamed to have the relations come, and she did till brought face to face with the fact that there were no more dollars to spend upon respectability, and that her quarters must hereafter conform to her earnings. She had been a dweller in that curious triangle, the remnant of "Greenwich village," the stronghold still of old New York, and she went at once to a region as unfamiliar to her conservative feet as Baxter or Hester, or any other street given over to evil. Far over toward the North River, in the first floor of a great tenement-house inhabited by the better class of Irish chiefly, she took two rooms, one a mere closet where the bed could stand; bestowed in them such furniture as remained, and at fifty, with no clew left that any friend could trace, began the fight for bread.

"It might have been better to go to the country," she said. "But you see I wasn't used to the country, and then any work I could get to do was right here. I'd always liked to sew, and so had Emeline, and we found we could get regular work on children's suits, with skirts and such things in the dull seasons. It was good pay, and we were comfortable till prices began to fall. We made fifteen dollars a week sometimes, and could have got ahead if it hadn't been for a little debt of my husband's that I wanted to pay, for we'd never owed anybody a penny and I couldn't let even that debt stand against his name. But when it was paid, somehow I came down with rheumatic fever, and I've never got back my full strength yet. And the prices kept going down. Emmy is an expert. I never knew her make a mistake, but working twelve and fourteen hours a day,—and it's 'most often fourteen,— the most she has made for more than a year and a half is eighty-five cents a day, and on that we've managed. I suppose we couldn't if I ever went out, but I've had no shoes in two years. I patch the ones I got then with one of my husband's old coats, and keep along, but we never get ahead enough for me to have shoes, and Emmy too, and she's the one that has to go out. How we live? It's all in this little book. It's foolish to put it down, and yet I always somehow liked to see how the money went, even when I had plenty, and it's second nature to put down every cent. Take last month. It had twenty-seven working days: $22.95. Out of that we took first the ten dollars for rent. I've been here eleven years, and they've raised a dollar on me twice. That leaves $12.95 for provisions and coal and light and clothes. 'Tisn't much for two people, is it? You wouldn't think it could be done, would you? Well, it is, and here's the expense for one week for what we eat:—

Sugar, 23; Tomatoes, 7; Potatoes, 5	$0.35
Tea, 15; Butter, 30; Bread, 12	0.57
Coal, 12; Milk, 15; Clams, 10	0.37
Oil, 15; Paper, 1; Clams, 10; Potatoes, 5	0.31
Cabbage, 5; Bread, 7; Flour, 15; Rolls, 3	0.30
Total	$1.90

"This week was an expensive one, for I got a pound of butter at once, but it will last into next week. And we had to have the scissors sharpened; that was five cents. There would have been five cents for wood, but you see they're building down the street, and one of the boys upstairs brought me a basketful of bits. You see there's no meat. We like it, but we only get a bit for Sundays sometimes. Emmy never wants much. Running a machine all day seems to take your appetite. But she likes clams; you see we had them twice, and I happened to read in the paper a good while ago that you could make soup of the water the cabbage was boiled in; a quart of the water and a cup of milk and a bit of butter and some flour to thicken. You wouldn't think it could be good, but it is, and it goes a good way. The coal ought not to be in with the food, ought it, unless it stays because I have to use it cooking? We oughtn't to spend so much on food, but I can't seem to make it less. Really, when you take out the coal and oil and the paper,—and we do want to see a paper sometimes,—it's only 1.62 for us both; eighty-one cents apiece; almost twelve cents a day, but I can't well seem to make it less. I call it twelve cents a day apiece. For the month that makes $7.44, and so you see there's $5.51 left. Then there are Emmy's car-fares when she goes out, for sometimes she works down-town and only evenings at home. Last month it was sixty cents a week, $2.70 for the month, and so there was just $2.81 left, and $1.50 of that went for shoes for Emmy. The month before, my hands weren't so stiff and I helped her a good deal, so we earned $26.70, and she got two remnants for $1.80 at Ehrich's and I made her a dress that looks very well. But she's nothing but patchwork underneath, and I'm the same, only worse. The coal is the trouble. By the scuttle it costs so much, and I try to get ahead and have a quarter of a ton at once, for there are places here to keep coal, but I never can. If it weren't for Emmy's missing me, it would be better for me to die, for I'm no use, you see, and times get no better, but worse. But I can't, and we must get along somehow. Lord help us all!"

"How could twelve cents' worth of coal do a week's cooking?"

"It couldn't. It didn't. I've a little oil stove that just boils the kettle, and tea and bread and butter what we have mostly. A gallon of oil goes a long way, and I can cook small things over it, too. The washing takes coal, and you see I must have soap and all that. I don't see how we could spend less. I've learned to manage even with what we get now, but there's a woman next door that I know better than anybody in this house,—for here it always seemed to me best to keep quite to myself for many reasons, but the chief that I'm always hoping for a change and a chance for Emmy. But this woman is a nice German woman that fell on the ice and sprained her ankle last winter, and we saw to her well as we could till she got better. She won't mind telling how she manages, but she's in the top of the house. She's a widow, and everybody dead belonging to her."

This house was a grade below the last in cleanliness, and children swarmed on stairs and in hall. Up to the fourth floor back; a ten-feet-square room, with one window, where, in spite of a defective sink in the hall, the odor from which seemed to penetrate and saturate everything, spotless cleanliness was the expression of every inch of space.

"Vy not?" the old woman said, when she understood my desire. "I tells you minc an' morc, too, for down de stairs I buy every day for the girl that is sick and goes out no more. If I quick were as girl I could save much, but I have sixty-five year. How shall I be quick? I earn forty-five, fifty cents sometime, but forty-five for day's work when I go as I can. An' so for week dat is $2.70; I can ten dollars a month, sometimes twelve dollars, and I pays three dollars for this room. To eat I will buy tea and our bread,—rye, for dat is stronger as your fine wheat. Tea is American, but I will not beer any more, since I see how women drinks it and de kinder, and it not like our beer but more tipsy. So I makes tea, and de cheese and de wurst is all not so much. It is de coal that is most. Vat I vill eat, he cost not so more as fifty cent; sometimes sixty, but I eat not ever all I could, for I must be warm a little, and dere is light, and to wash, and some shoe. It is bad to be big as I, for shoe not last. But a loaf of bread, five cents, do all day and some in next; and cheese a pound is ten, if I have him; and wurst is fifteen, for sometime he is best, and a pound stay a week if I not greedy. Tea will be thirty cents, but he is good a month, and sugar a pound, two pound sometime, but butter no, and milk a cent for Sunday. So I live, and I beg not. Can I more? I thank the good God only that there is no more Hans or Lisa or any to be hungry with me. It is good they go."

"And you buy for some one else?"

"Oh ja, but she will die soon and care not. It is de kinder that care. Two, and one six and one eight and cannot earn. She sew all day on machine. It is babies' cloaks, so vite and nice. In two days she will make dree, for see, dere is two linings and cape and cuff is all scallop, and she must stitch first and then bind and hem. All is hem, all over inside, so nice, and she make dem so nice. But eight dollars a dozen is all, and it is a week for nine, and so she get not more as five dollars because she is sick and must stop. And there is the grandvater that is old, and de kinder and she and all must live. Rent is $5.50, dat I know, and I pay for her dis week $1.60 for bread and tea and potatoes and some milk, and molasses for de kinder on bread, and butter a little, and milk, but not meat. It is de grandvater eat too much, but how shall one help it? De rest is clothes for all, but dere is no shoe for de kinder, and I see not if dere will be shoe. How shall it be?"

One after another the cases on the west side gave in their testimony. Save in the first one there were no formal accounts. But a little thinking brought out the items,—for many baker's bread, tea, sugar, a little milk, and butter and a bit of meat once or twice a week, the average cost of food per head for the majority of cases being ninety cents per week. All coal was bought by the scuttle, a scuttle of medium size counting as twelve cents' worth, thus much more than doubling the cost per ton. In the same way, wood by the bundle and oil by the quart gave the utmost margin of profit to the seller, and the same fact applied to all provisions sold. In no case save the one first mentioned, where the mother had learned that cabbage-water can form the basis for a nourishing and very palatable soup, was there the faintest gleam of understanding that the same amount of money could furnish a more varied, more savory, and more nourishing regimen.

"Beans!" said one indignant soul. "What time have I to think of beans, or what money to buy coal to cook 'em? What you'd want if you sat over a machine fourteen hours a day would be tea like lye to put a back-bone in you. That's why we have tea always in the pot, and it don't make much odds what's with it. A slice of bread is about all. Once in a while you get ragin', tearin' hungry. Seems as if you'd swallow teapot or anything handy to fill up like, but that ain't often—lucky for us!"

"If you all clubbed together, couldn't one cook for you,—make good soup and oatmeal and things that are nourishing? You would be stronger then."

"Stronger for what? More hours at the machine? More grinding your own flesh and bones into flour for them that's over us? Ma'am, it's easy to see you mean well, an' I won't say but what you know more than some that comes around what you're talkin' about. Club we might. I'm not denying it could be done, if there was time; but who of us has the time even if she'd the will? I was never much hand for cookin'. We'd our tea an' bread an' a good bit of fried beef or pork, maybe, when my husband was alive an' at work. He cared naught for fancy things like beans an' such. It's the tea that keeps you up, an' as long as I can get that I'll not bother about beans."

In the same house an old Swiss woman, who had fallen from her first estate as lady's maid through one grade and another of service, was ending her days on a wage of two dollars per week, earned in a suspender factory, where she sewed on buckles. In her case marriage with a drinking husband had eaten up both her savings and her earnings, and age now prevented her taking up household service, which she ranked as most comfortable and most profitable. But she had been taught while almost a child to cook, and though her expenditure for food was a little below a dollar per week, the savory smell from a saucepan on her tiny stove showed that she had something more nearly like nourishment than her neighbors.

"I try sometimes to teach," she said. "I give some of my soup, and they eat it and say it is good, but they not stop to do so much dat is fuss. All this in the saucepan is seven cents,—three cents for bones and some bits the kind butcher trow in, and the rest vegetable and barley. But it makes me two days. I have lentils, too, yes, and beans, and plenty things to flavor, and I buy rye bread and coffee to Sunday. Never tea, oh, no! Tea is so vicket. It make hand shake and head fly all round. Good soup is best, and more when one can. Vegetable is many and salad, and when I make more dollar I buy some egg. But not tea; not big loaf of white bread dot swell and swell inside and ven it is gone leave one all so empty. I would teach many but they like it not. They want only de tea; always de tea."

"De tea" and the sewing-machine are naturally inseparable allies, and so long as the sewing-women must work fourteen hours daily they will remain so; the rank fluid retarding digestion and thus proving as friendly an aid as the "bone" which the half-fed Irish peasant demands in his potato. For the west side the story was quite plain, but for such returns as the east side has to offer there is still room for further detail.

CHAPTER ELEVENTH.

UNDER THE BRIDGE AND BEYOND.

BETWEEN east and west side poverty and its surroundings exists always this difference, that the west is newer and thus escapes the inherited miseries that hedge about life in such regions as the Fourth Ward. There, where old New York once centred, and where Dutch gables and dormer windows may still be seen, is not only the foulness of the present, each nationality in the swarming tenements representing a distinct type of dirt and a distinct method of dealing with it and in it, but the foulness also of the past, in decay and mould and crumbling wall and all silent forces of destruction at work here for a generation and more. Those of us who have watched the evolution of the Fourth Ward into some show of decency recognize many causes as having worked toward the same end; yet even when one notes to-day the changes wrought, first by business, the march of which has wiped out many former landmarks, setting in their place great warehouses and factories, and then of philanthropy, which, as in the case of Miss Collins's tenements, has transformed dens into some semblance of homes, there remains the conviction that dens are uppermost still. The business man hurrying down Fulton or Beekman Street, the myriads who pass up and down in the various east-side car lines, with those other myriads who cross the great Bridge, have small conception what thousands are packed away in the great tenements, and the rookeries even more crowded, or what depth of vileness flaunts itself openly when day is done and the creatures of shadow come out to the light that for many quarters is the only sunshine. This ward has had minute and faithful description from one of the most energetic of workers for better sanitary conditions among the poor,—Mr. Charles Wingate, whose admirable papers on "Tenement House Life," published by the "Tribune" in 1884-1885, must be regarded as authority for the sanitary phases of the question. Little by little these have bettered, till the death rate has come within normal limits and the percentage of crime ceased to represent the largest portion of the inhabitants. Yet here, on this familiar battle-ground, civilization and something worse than mere barbarism still struggle. For which is the victory?

Under the great Bridge, whose piers have taken the place of much that was foulest in the Fourth Ward, stands a tenement-house so shadowed by the structure that, save at midday, natural light barely penetrates it. The inhabitants are of all grades and all nationalities. The men are chiefly 'longshoremen, working intermittently on the wharves, varying this occupation by long seasons of drinking, during which every pawnable article vanishes, to be gradually redeemed or altogether lost, according to the energy with which work is resumed. The women scrub offices, peddle fruit or small office necessities, take in washing, share, many of them, in the drinking bouts, and are, as a whole, content with brutishness, only vaguely conscious of a wretchedness that, so long as it is intermittent, is no spur to reform of methods. The same roof covers many who yield to none of these temptations, but are working patiently; some of them widows with children that must be fed; a few solitary, but banding with neighbors in cloak or pantaloon making, or the many forms of slop-work in the hands of sweaters. Sunshine has no place in these rooms which no enforced laws have made decent, and where occasional individual effort has power against the unspeakable filth ruling in tangible and intangible forms, sink and sewer and closet uniting in a common and all-pervading stench. The chance visitor has sometimes to rush to the outer air, deadly sick and faint at even a breath of this noisomeness. The most determined one feels inclined to burn every garment worn during such quest, and wonders if Abana or Pharpar or even Jordan itself could carry healing and cleansing in their floods.

The dark halls have other uses than as receptacles for refuse or filth. Hiding behind doors or in corners, or, grown bolder, seeking no concealment, children hardly more than babies teach one another such new facts of foulness as may so far have chanced to escape them,—baby voices reciting a ritual of oaths and obscenity learned in this Inferno, which, could it have place by Dante's, might be better known to a cultured generation. Only a Zola could describe deliberately what any eye may see, but any minute detail of which would excite an outburst of popular indignation. Yet I am by no means certain that such detail has not far more right to space than much that fills our morning papers, and that the plain bald statement of facts, shorn of all flights of fancy or play of facetiousness, might not rouse the public to some sense of what lies below the surface of this fair-seeming civilization of to-day. Not alone in the shadow of the great pier, but wherever men and women must herd like brutes, these things exist and shape the little lives that missions do not, and as yet cannot, reach, and that we prefer to deal with later, when actual violation of laws has placed them in the hands of the State. Work as she may, the woman who must find home for herself and children in such surroundings is powerless to protect them from the all-pervading foulness. They may escape a portion of the actual degradation. They can never escape a knowledge the possibility of which is unknown to what we call barbarism, but part and parcel of the daily life of civilization.

Granted instantly that only the lowest order of worker must submit to such conditions, yet we have seen that this lowest order is legion; that its numbers increase with every day; and that no Board of Health or of Sanitary Inspectors has yet been able to alter, save here and there, the facts that are a portion of the tenement-house system.

It is chiefly with the house under the Bridge that we deal at present. Its upper rooms hold many workers whose testimony has helped to make plain how the east side lives. Little by little, as the blocks of granite swung into place and the pier grew, the sunshine vanished, its warmth and light replaced by the electric glow, cold and hard and blinding. The day's work has ceased to be the day's work, and the women who cannot afford the gas or oil that must burn if they work in the daytime, sleep while day lasts, and when night comes and the electric light penetrates every corner of the shadowy rooms, turn to the toil by which their bread is won. Never was deeper satire upon the civilization of which we boast. Natural law, natural living, abolished once for all, and this light that blinds but holds no cheer shining upon the mass of weary humanity who have forgotten what sunshine may mean and who know no joy that life was meant to hold!

In one of these rooms, clean, if cleanliness were possible where walls and ceiling and every plank and beam reek with the foulness from sewer and closet, three women were at work on overalls. Two machines were placed directly under the windows to obtain every ray of light. The room, ten by twelve feet, with a small one half the size opening from it, held a small stove, the inevitable teapot steaming at the back; a table with cups and saucers and a loaf of bread still uncut; and a small dresser in one corner, in which a few dishes were ranged. A sickly geranium grew in an old tomato-can, but save for this the room held no faintest attempt at adornment of any sort. In many of them the cheapest colored prints are pinned up, and in one, one side had been decorated with all the trademarks peeled from the goods on which the family worked. Here there was no time for even such attempts at betterment. The machines rushed on as we talked, with only a momentary pause as interest deepened, and one woman nodded confirmation to the statement of another.

"We've clubbed, so's to get ahead a little," said the finisher, whose fingers flew as she made buttonholes in the waistband and flap of the overalls. "We were each in a room by ourselves, but after the fever, when the children died and I hadn't but two left, it seemed as if we'd be more sensible to all go in together and see if we couldn't be more comfortable. We'd have left anyway, and tried for a better place, but for one thing,—we hadn't time to move; and for another, queer as it seems, you get used to even the worst places and feel as if you couldn't change. We'll have to, if the landlord doesn't do something about the closets. It's no good telling the agent, and I don't know as anybody in the house knows just who the landlord is. Anyway, the smell's enough to kill you sometimes, and it's a burning disgrace that human beings have to live in such a pig-pen. It's cheap rent. We pay five dollars a month for this place. When I came here it was from a neck-tie place over on Allen Street, that's moved now, and my husband was mate on a tug and earned well. But he took to drink and sold off everything I'd brought with me, and at last he was hurt in a fight round the corner, and died in hospital of gangrene. Mary's husband there was a bricklayer and had big wages, but he drank them fast as he made them, and he was ugly when the drink was in, which mine wasn't. But there's hardly one in this house, man or woman, that don't take a drop to keep off the fever; and even I, that hate the sight or smell of it, I wake up in the morning with an awful kind o' goneness that seems as if a taste might help it. The tea stops that, though. Tea's the best friend we've got. We'd never stand it if it wasn't for tea."

"Are overalls steady pay through the year?"

"There's nothing that's steady, so far as I can find out, but want and misery. Just now overalls are up; the Lord only knows why, for you never can tell what'll be up and what down. They're up, and we're making a dollar a dozen on these. I have done a dozen a day, but it's generally ten. There's the long seams, and the two pockets, and the buckle strap and the waistband and three buttonholes, and the stays and the finishing. They're heavy machines too, and take the backbone right out of you before night comes. But you sleep like the dead, that's one comfort. It would be more if you didn't have to wake more than they do. When the overall rush is over, it'll be back to pants again. That's my trade. I learned it regular after I was married, when I saw Tim wasn't going to be any dependence. There were the children then, and I thought I'd send 'em to school and keep things decent maybe. I know all about pants, the best and the worst, but it's mostly worse these days. First the German women piled in ready to do your work for half your rates, and when they'd got well started, in comes the Italians and cuts under, till it's a wonder anybody keeps soul and body together."

"We don't," one of the women said, turning suddenly. "I got rid o' my soul long ago, such as 'twas. Who's got time to think about souls, grinding away here fourteen hours a day to turn out contract goods? 'Tain't souls that count. It's bodies that can be driven, an' half starved an' driven still, till they drop in their tracks. I'm driving now to pay a doctor's bill for my three that went with the fever. Before that I was driving to put food into their mouths. I never owed a cent to no man. I've been honest and paid as I went and done a good turn when I could. If I'd chosen the other thing while I'd a pretty face of my own I'd a had ease and comfort and a quick death. Such life as this isn't living."

The machine whirled on as she ended, to make up the time lost in her outburst. The finisher shook her head as she looked at her, then poured a cup of tea and put it silently on the edge of the table where it could be reached.

"She's right enough," she said, "but there's no use thinking about it. I try to sometimes, just to see if there's any way out, but there isn't. I've even said I'd take a place; but I don't know anything about housework, and who'd take one looking as I do, and not a rag that's fit to be put on? I cover up in an old waterproof when I go for work. They wouldn't give it to me if they saw my dress in rags below, and me with no time to mend it. But we're doing better than some. We've had meat twice this week, and we've kept warm. It's the coal that eats up your money,—twelve cents a scuttle, and no place to keep more if ever we got ahead enough to get more at a time. It's lucky that tea's so staying. Give me plenty of tea, and the most I want generally besides is bread and a scrape of butter. It's all figured out. It's long since I've spent more than seventy-five cents a week for what I must eat. I've no time to cook even if I had anything, so it's lucky I haven't. I suppose there'd be plenty to eat if you once made up your mind to take a place."

It was the second machine that stopped now, and the haggard woman running it faced about suddenly. "Do you know what come to my girl," she said,—"my girl that I brought up decent and that was a good girl? I said to myself a trade was no good, for it was more an' more starvation wages, and I'd put her with folks that would be good to her, even if the other girls did look down on her for going into service. She was fifteen, and a still little thing with soft eyes and a pretty, soft way, if she did come of a drinking father. I put her with a lady that wanted a waitress and said she'd train her well. She'd three boarders in the house, and all gentlemen to look at, and one that's in a bank to-day he did his best to turn her head on the sly, and when he found he couldn't, one Sunday when she was alone in the house and none to hear or help, he had his will. The mistress turned her off the hour she heard it, for Nettie went to her when she come home. 'Such things don't happen unless the girl is to blame,' she said. 'Never show your shameless face here again.' Nettie came home to me kind of dazed, and she stayed dazed till she went to a hospital and a baby was born dead, and she dead herself a week after. An' it isn't one time alone or my girl alone. It's over an' over an' over that that thing happens. There's plenty that go to the bad of their own free will, but I know plenty more with the same chance that doesn't, an' there's many a mother that's been in service herself that says, 'Whatever the mistress may know about it she can't tell, but the devil's let loose when the master or a son maybe is around, an' they'll not have their girls standing what they had to stand and then turned off without a character because they were found with the master talkin' to 'em.' It's women that keeps women down an' is hard on 'em. I'll take my chances with any Jew you'll bring along before I'll put myself in the power of women that calls themselves ladies an' hasn't as much heart as a broomstick; an' I'll warn every girl to keep to herself an' learn a trade, an' not run the risk she'll run if she goes out to service, letting alone the way you're looked down on."

There was no time for discussion. The machines must go on; but, as usual, much more than the fact of which I was in search had come to me, and, strangely enough, in this house and in others of its kind inspected one after another, much the same story was told. In the "improved tenements" close at hand, where comparative comfort reigned, more than one woman gave willingly the detail of the weekly expenditure for food, and added, as if the underlying question had made itself felt, "It's betther to be a little short even an' your own misthress," with other words that have their place elsewhere. On the upper floor of one of these houses a pantaloon-maker sat in a fireless room, finishing the last of a dozen which when taken back would give her money for coal and food. She had been ill for three days, and on the bed,—an old mattress on a dry-goods box in the corner. "Even that's more than I had for a good while," she said. "I'd pawned everything before my husband died, except the machine. I couldn't make but twenty-two cents a pair on the pants, an' as long as he could hold up he did the pressing. With him to help a little I made three a day. That seems little, but there was so many pieces to each pair,—side and watch and pistol pockets, buckle strap, waistband, and bottom facings and lap; six buttonholes and nine buttons. We lived—I don't just know how we lived. He was going in consumption an' very set about it. 'I'll have no medicine an' no doctor to make me hang an' drag along,' he says. 'I've got to go, an' I know it, an' I'll do it as fast as I can.' He was Scotch, an' took his porridge to the last, but I came to loathe the sight of it. He could live on six cents a day. I couldn't. 'I'm the kind for your contractors,' he'd say. 'It's a glorious country, and the rich'll be richer yet when there's more like me.' He didn't mind what he said, an' when a Bible-reader put her head in one day, 'Come in,' he says. 'My wife's working for a Christian contractor at sixty-six cents a day, an' I'm what's left of another Christian's dealings with me, keeping me as a packer in a damp basement and no fire. Come in and let's see what more Christianity has to say about it.' He scared her, his eyes was so shiny an' he most gone then. But there's many a one that doesn't go over fifty cents a week for what she'll eat. God help them that's starving us all by bits, if there is a God, but I'm doubting it, else why don't things get better, an' not always worse an' worse?"

For east and west, however conditions might differ, the final word was the same, and it stands as the summary of the life that is lived from day to day by these workers,—"never better, always worse and worse."

CHAPTER TWELFTH.

ONE OF THE FUR-SEWERS.

"I SUPPOSE if you'd been born on the top of a hill in New Hampshire with the stones so thick ten miles of stone wall couldn't have used 'em up, an' the steeple of the Methodist meetin'-house the only thing in sight, maybe you'd have wanted to get where you could see folks too. It was just Elkins luck to have another hill between us an' the village so't I couldn't see beyond the woods between. If there was a contrary side to anything it always fell to father, an' I'm some like him, though I've got mother's way of never knowing when I'm knocked flat, though I've had times enough to find out. But I said straight through, 'If ever there's a chance of getting to New York I'll take it. Boston won't do. I want the biggest an' the stirringest thing there is in the United States,' an' Leander felt just as I did.

"Leander lived down the valley a way, an' such cobble-stones as hadn't come to our share had come to his. He'd laid wall from the time he was ten years old, and he'd sat on the hay an' cried for pure lonesomeness. His folks weren't any hands to talk, an' he couldn't even have the satisfaction of meetin' Sundays, because they was Seventh Day Baptists, an' so set a minister couldn't get near 'em. An' Leander was conscientious an' thought he ought to stay by. I didn't. I told him from the time we went to school together that I was bound to get to New York, an' that sort of fired him up, an' we've talked hours to time about what it was like, an' what we'd do if we ever got there. My folks were set against the notion, an' so were his, but he went after a while, with some man that was up in the summer an' that gave him a place in a store. I couldn't go on account of father's dying sudden an' mother's holdin' on harder'n ever to me, but she was took within the year, an' there I was, free enough, an' not a soul in the world but Leander's folks that seemed to think much one way or another how I was likely to come out.

"There was a mortgage on the farm, an' Dr. Grayson foreclosed an' had most of the money for his bill; an' when things were all settled I had forty dollars in cash an' the old furniture. Leander's folks was dreadful short for things, for they'd been burned out once, an' so I just turned everything over to them but some small things I could pack in my trunk, mother's teaspoons an' such, an' walked down to the village an' took the stage for Portsmouth. I wasn't scared. I didn't care nor think how I looked. It was heaven to think I was on the way to folks an' the things folks do. I ain't given to crying, but that day I sat back in the stage an' cried just for joy to think I was going to have something different.

"All this time I hadn't thought much what I'd do. Forty dollars seemed a big lot, enough for weeks ahead. I'd done most everything about a house, an' I could make everything I wore. I had only to look at a pattern an' I could go home an cut out one like it. The dress I had on was cheap stuff, but when I looked at other folks's I saw it wasn't so much out o' the way. So I said, most likely some dressmaker would take me, an' I'd try my luck that way. This was before I got to Boston, an' I went round there all the afternoon before it was time to take the train, for the conductor told me just what to do, an' I hadn't a mite of trouble. I never do going to a strange place. I was half a mind to stay in Boston when I saw the Common an' the crowds of folks. I sat still there an' just looked at 'em, an' cried again for joy to think I'd got where there were so many. 'But there'll be more in New York,' I said, 'an' there'll be sure to be plenty ready to do a good turn.' I could have hugged 'em all. I didn't think then the time would ever come that I'd hate the sight of faces an' wish myself on top of the hill in the cobble-stones, but it did, an' it does now sometimes.

"I went on board the boat that night sort of crazy. I'd gone an' got some sandwiches an' things at a place the conductor told me, an' I sat on the deck in the moonlight an' ate my supper. I'd been too happy to eat before, an' I was so happy then I could hardly keep still. There was a girl not far off, a kind of nice-looking girl, an' she watched me, an' at last she began to talk. In half an hour I knew all about her an' she about me. She was a Rhode Island girl an' had worked in a mill near Providence, an' gone to New York at last an' learned fur-sewing. She said it was a good trade, an' she made ten an' twelve dollars a week while the season lasted an' never less than five. This seemed a mint of money, an' when she said one of their old hands had died, an' she could take me right in as her friend an' teach me herself, I felt as if my fortune was made.

"Well, I went with her next day. She had a room in Spring Street, near Hudson,—an old-fashioned house that belonged to two maiden sisters, an' I went in with her the first night, an' afterward for a while had the hall bedroom. It didn't take me long to learn. It was a Jew place an' there were thirty girls, but he treated us well. For my part I've fared just as well with Jews as ever I did with Christians, an' sometimes better. I'd taken to Hattie so that I couldn't bear to think of leaving her, an' so I let my dressmaking plan go. But I'll tell you what I found out in time. These skins are all dressed with arsenic. The dealers say there's nothing poisonous about them, but of course they lie. Every pelt has more or less in it, an' the girls show it just as the artificial-flower girls show it. Your eyelids get red an' the lids all puffy, an' you're white as chalk. The dealers say the red eyes come from the flying hairs. Perhaps they do, but the lids don't, an' every fur-sewer is poisoned a little with every prick of her needle. What the flying hair does is just to get into your throat an' nose and everywhere, an' tickle till you cough all the time, an' a girl with weak lungs hasn't a chance. The air is full of fur, an' then the work-room is kept tight shut for fear of moths getting in. The work is easy enough. It's just an everlasting patchwork, for you're always sewing together little bits, hundreds of them, that you have to match. You sew over an' over with linen thread, an' you're always piecing out an' altering shapes. It's nothing to sew up a thing when you've once got it pieced together. If it's beaver, all the long hairs must be picked out, an' it's the same with sealskin. We made up everything; sable an' Siberian squirrel, bear, fox, marten, mink, otter, an' all the rest. There were some girls very slow in learning that only got a dollar a week, an' in the end four, but most of them can average about five. I was seventeen when I began, an' in a year I had caught all the knack there is to it, an' was an expert, certain of ten dollars in the season an' about six in between. It's generally piece-work, with five or six months when you can earn ten or twelve dollars even, an' the rest of the time five or six dollars. In the busiest times there'd be fifty girls perhaps, but this was only for two or three months, an' then they discharged them. 'Tisn't a trade I'd ever let a girl take up if I could help it; I suppose somebody's got to do it, but there ought to be higher wages for those that do.

"This went on five years. I won't take time telling about Leander, but he'd got to be a clerk at Ridley's an' had eight hundred dollars a year, an' we'd been engaged for two years, an' just waiting to see if he wouldn't get another rise. I knew we could manage on that. Leander was more ambitious than me. He said we ought to live in a showy boarding-house an' make our money tell that way, but I told him I was used to the Spring Street house, an' we could have a whole floor an' be snug as could be an' Hattie board with us. He gave in, an' it's well he did; for we hadn't been married six months before he had a hemorrhage an' just went into quick consumption. I'd kept right on with my trade, but I was pulled down myself an' my eyelids so swollen sometimes I could hardly see out of 'em. But I got a sewing-machine from money I'd saved, an' I took in work from a place on Canal Street,—a good one, too, that always paid fair. The trouble was my eyes. I'd used 'em up, an' they got so I couldn't see the needle nor sew straight, an' had to give up the sewing, an' then I didn't know which way to turn, for there was Leander. The old folks were up there still, wrastling with the stones, but poorer every year, an' I couldn't get him up there. Leander was patient as a saint, but he fretted over me an' how I was to get along.

"'You're not to worry,' says I. 'There's more ways than one of earning, an' if my eyes is bad, I've got two hands an' know how to use 'em. I'll take a place an' do housework if I can't do nothing else.'

"You'd never believe how the thought o' that weighed on him. He'd wake me up in the night to say, 'Now, Almiry, jest give up that thought an' promise me you'll try something else. I think I'd turn in my grave if I had to know you was slavin' in anybody's kitchen.'

"'What's the odds?' I said. 'You have to be under orders whatever you do. I think it won't be a bad change from the shop.'

"He took on so, though, that to quiet him I promised him I wouldn't do it unless I had to, an' 'twasn't long after that that he died. Between the doctor's bill—an' he was a kind man, I will say, an' didn't charge a tenth of what he had ought to—an' the funeral an' all, I was cleaned out of everything. I'd had to pawn a month before he died, an' was just stripped. Sewing was no good. My eyes went back on me like everything else, an' in a fortnight I knew there wasn't anything for it but getting a place. I left such things as I had in charge of the old ladies an' answered an advertisement for 'a capable girl willing to work.'

"Well, it was a handsome house an' elegant things in the parlors an' bedrooms, but my heart sunk when she took me into the kitchen. The last girl had gone off in a rage an' left everything, an' there was grease and dirt from floor to ceiling. It was a deep basement, with one window an' a door opening right into the area with glass set in it, an' iron bars to both; but dirty to that degree you couldn't see three feet beyond; cockroaches walking round at their ease an' water-bugs so thick you didn't know where to lay anything.

"'You'll have things quite your own way,' the lady said, 'for I never come into the kitchen. Bridget attends to upstairs, but you attend to fires and the meals and washing and ironing, and I expect punctuality and everything well done.'

"'At least it sounds independent,' I thought, and I made up my mind to try it, for the wages were fifteen dollars a month, an' that with board seemed doing well. Bridget came down presently. She was seventeen an' a pretty girl rather, but she looked fit to drop, an' fell down in a chair.

"'It's the bell,' she said. 'The comin' an' goin' here niver ceases, an' whin 'tisn't the front door it's her own bell, an' she'll jingle it or holler up the tube in the middle o' the night if she takes a notion.'

"I wouldn't ask questions, for I thought I should find out soon enough, so I said I'd like to go up to my room a minute.

"'It's our room you'll mane,' she said. 'There's but the one, an' it's hard enough for two to be slapin' on a bed that's barely the width o' one.'

"My heart sank then, for I'd always had a place that was comfortable all my life, but it sunk deeper when I went up there. A hall bedroom, with a single bed an' a small table, with a washbowl an' small pitcher, one chair an' some nails in the door for hanging things; that was all except a torn shade at the window. I looked at the bed. The two ragged comfortables were foul with long use. I thought of my nice bed down at Spring Street, my own good sheets an' blankets an' all, an' I began to cry.

"'You don't look as if you was used to the likes of it,' Bridget said. 'There's another room the same as this but betther. Why not ax for it?'

"I started down the stairs an' came right upon Mrs. Melrose, who smiled as if she thought I had been enjoying myself.

"'I'm perfectly willing to try an' do your work as well as I know how,' I said, 'but I must have a place to myself an' clean things in it.'

"'Highty-tighty!' says she. 'What impudence is this? You'll take what I give you and be thankful to get it. Plenty as good as you have slept in that room and never complained.'

"'Then it's time some one did,' I said. 'I don't ask anything but decency, an' if you can't give it I must try elsewhere.'

"'Then you'd better set about it at once,' she says, an' with that I bid her good-afternoon an' walked out. I had another number in my pocket, an' I went straight there; an' this time I had sense enough to ask to see my room. It was bare enough, but clean. There were only three in the family, an' it was a little house on Perry Street. There I stayed two years. They were strange years. The folks were set in their ways an' they had some money. But every day of that time the lady cut off herself from the meat what she thought I ought to have, an' ordered me to put away the rest. She allowed no dessert except on Sunday, an' she kept cake and preserves locked in an upstairs closet. I wouldn't have minded that. What I did mind was that from the time I entered the house till I left it there was never a word for me beyond an order, any more than if I hadn't been a human being. She couldn't find fault. I was born clean, an' that house shone from top to bottom; but a dog would have got far more kindness than they gave me. At last I said I'd try a place where there were children an' maybe they'd like me. Mrs. Smith was dumb with surprise when I told her I must leave. 'Leave!' she says. 'We're perfectly satisfied. You're a very good girl, Almira.' 'It's the first time you've ever told me so,' I says, 'an' I think a change is best all round.' She urged, but I was set, an' I went from there when the month was up.

"Well, my eyes stayed bad for sewing, an' I must keep on at housework. I've been in seven places in six years. I could have stayed in every one, an' about every one I could tell you things that make it plain enough why a self-respecting girl would rather try something else. I don't talk or think nonsense about wanting to be one of the family. I don't. I'd much rather keep to myself. But out of these seven places there was just one in which the mistress seemed to think I was a human being with something in me the same as in her. I've been underfed an' worked half to death in two of the houses. The mistress expected just so much, an' if it failed she stormed an' went on an' said I was a shirk an' good for nothing an' all that. There was only one of them that had a decently comfortable room or that thought to give me a chance at a book or paper now an' then. As long as I had a trade I was certain of my evenings an' my Sundays. Now I'm never certain of anything. I'm not a shirk. I'm quick an' smart, an' I know I turn off work. In ten hours I earn more than I ever get. But I begin my day at six an' in summer at five, an' it's never done before ten an' sometimes later. This place I'm in now seems to have some kind of fairness about it, an' Mrs. Henshaw said yesterday, 'You can't tell the comfort it is to me, Almira, to have some one in the house I can trust. I hope you will be comfortable an' happy enough to stay with us.' 'I'll stay till you tell me to go,' I says, an' I meant it. My little room looks like home an' is warm and comfortable. My kitchen is bright an' light, an' she's told me always to use the dining-room in the evenings for myself an' for friends. She tries to give me fair hours. If there were more like her there'd be more willing for such work, but she's the first one I've heard of that tries to be just. That's something that women don't know much about. When they do there'll be better times all round."

Here stands the record of a woman who has become invaluable to the family she serves, but whose experiences before this harbor was reached include every form of oppression and even privation. Many more of the same nature are recorded and are arranging themselves under heads, the whole forming an unexpected and formidable arraignment of household service in its present phases. This arraignment bides its time, but while it waits it might be well for the enthusiastic prescribers of household service as the easy and delightful solution of the working-woman's problem to ask how far it would be their own choice if reduced to want, and what justice for both sides is included in their personal theory of the matter.

CHAPTER THIRTEENTH.

SOME DIFFICULTIES OF AN EMPLOYER WHO EXPERIMENTED.

THE business face in the great cities is assimilating to such degree that all men are brothers in a sense and to an extent unrealized by themselves. Competition has deepened lines, till one type of the employer in his first estate, while the struggle is still active and success uncertain, loses not only youth and freshness, but with them, too often, any token of owning a soul capable of looking beyond the muckrake by which money is drawn in. If he acquires calm and graciousness, it is the calmness of subtlety and the graciousness of the determined schemer, who, finding every man's hand practically against him, arranges his own life on the same basis, and wages war against the small dealer or manufacturer below and the monopolist above, his one passionate desire being to escape from the ranks of the first and find his name enrolled among the last. He retains a number of negative virtues. He is, as a rule, "an excellent provider" where his own family is concerned, and he is kind beyond those limits if he has time for it. He would not deliberately harm man or woman who serves him; but to keep even with his competitors—if possible, to get beyond them—demands and exhausts every energy, leaving none to spare for other purposes. Such knowledge as comes from perpetual contact with the grasping, scheming side of humanity is his in full. As the fortune grows and ease becomes certain, a well-fed, well-groomed look replaces the eager sharpness of the early days. He may at this stage turn to horses as the most positive source of happiness. He is likely also, with or without this tendency, to acquire a taste for art, measuring its value by what it costs, and to plan for himself a house representing the utmost that money can buy. But the house and its treasures is, after all, but a mausoleum, and the grave it covers holds the man that might have been. Life in its larger meanings has remained a sealed book, and the gold counted as chief good becomes at last an impenetrable barrier between him and any knowledge of what might have been his portion. He is content, and remains content till the end, and that new beginning in which the starved soul comes to the first consciousness of its own most desperate and pitiful poverty.

This for one type, and a type more and more common with every year of the system in which competition is king. But here and there one finds another,—that of the man whose conscience remains sensitive, no matter what familiarity with legalized knavery may come, and who ponders the question of what he owes to those by whose aid his fortune is made. Nor is he the employer who evades the real issue by a series of what he calls benefactions, and who organizes colonies for his work-people, in which may be found all the charm of the feudal system, and an underlying despotism no less feudal. He would gladly make his workers copartners with him were intelligence enough developed among them to admit such action, and he experiments faithfully and patiently.

It is such an employer whose own words best give the story he has to tell. It is not an American that speaks but a German Jew,—a title often the synonyme for depths of trickery, but more often than is known meaning its opposite in all points. Keen sagacity rules, it is true, but there is also a large and tender nature, sorrowing with the sorrow of humanity and seeking anxiously some means by which that sorrow may lessen. A small manufacturer, fighting his way against monopoly, he is determinately honest in every thread put into his goods, in every method of his trade; his face shrewd yet gentle and wise,—a face that child or woman would trust, and the business man be certain he could impose upon until some sudden turn brought out the shrewdness and the calm assurance of absolute knowledge in his own lines. For thirty years and more his work has held its own, and he has made for himself a place in the trade that no crisis can affect. His own view of the situation is distinctly serious, but even for him there was a flickering smile as he recalled some passages of the experience given here in part. His English limps slightly at moments of excitement, but his mastery of its shades of meaning never, and this is his version of the present relation between employer and employed:—

"In me always are two peoples,—one that loves work well, that must work ever to be happy, and one that will think and think ever how hard is life even with work that is good and with much to love. In village or in city, for I begin with one and go on to the other, in both alike it is work always that is too much; long hours when strength is gone and there should be rest, but when always man and woman, yes, and child, must go on for the little more that more hours will earn. For myself, I want not what is called pleasure when the day is done. A book that is good contents me, and is friend and amusement in one. But as I love a book more and more, and desire more time to be with them, I begin first to think, why should so many hours be given to work that there are none in which men have strength or time or desire left for something that is better? These things I think much of before I come to America. I have my trade from my father and his father. We are silk-weavers from the time silk is known, but for myself I have chosen ribbons, and it is ribbons I make all my life and that my son will make after me.

"At first when I come here to this country that for years I hope for and must not reach, because I am held to my father who is old—at first I have little money and can only be with another who manufactures. But already some dishonesties have come in. The colors are not firm; the silk has weight given it, so that more body than is belongs to the ribbon; there is an inch, maybe, cut short in the lengths. There is every way to make the most and give the least. And there is something that from the days I begin to think at all, seems ever injustice and wrong. Side by side it may be, men and women work together at the looms; but for the women it is half, sometimes two thirds, what the man can earn, yet the work the same. This is something to alter when time is ripe, and at last it is come. I have saved as I earned and added to what I bring with me, and I buy for myself the plant of a man who retires, and get me a place, this place where I am, and that changes little. His workers come with me,—a few, for I begin with four looms only, but soon have seven, and so go on. At first I think only of how I may shorten hours and make time for them to rest and learn what they will, but a good friend of mine from the beginning is doctor, and as I go on he speaks to me much of things I should do for health. And then I think of them and study, and I see that there is much I have never learned and that they must learn also with me.

"There is one thing that Americans will, more than all peoples of the earth. They will have a place so hot that breath is nowhere, and women more even than men. I begin to think how I shall keep them warm yet give them to breathe. The place is old, as you see. No builder thought ever of air in such time as this was built, and if they think to-day, it is chiefly wrong, for in all places I go one breathes the breath of all others, never true air of heaven. At first I open windows from top and before they come; but when they see it they cry out and say, 'O Mr. B——! You want to freeze us!' 'Not so,' I say; 'I would make you healthy.' And they say, 'We're healthy enough. We don't want draughts.' It is true. There were draughts, and I begin to think how this shall be changed, and try many things, and all of them they pull down or push out or stop up tight, whichever way will most surely abolish air. At last I bring up my doctor who is wise and can explain better than I, and I say that work may stop and all listen and learn. They listen but they laugh, all but one, and say, 'How funny! What is use of so much fuss?'

"While I do these things which I keep on and will not stop, finding best at last a shaft and a hole above, that they cannot pull out or reach to fill, I think of other things. They eat at noon what they bring,—pie that is dear to Americans, and small cakes, many of them; but good bread that has nourishment, or good drink like soup or coffee, no. They stand many hours and: faint and weak. So I say there must be good coffee for them, and I tell them, 'Girls, I will buy a big urn and there shall be coffee and milk, and for two cents you have a big cup so sweet as you will, or if you like better it shall be hot soup.' Above in a room was a a Swiss that knew good soup, and that would, if I pay her a little, buy all that is wanted and a make a big pot, so that each could have a bowl. This also I would have them pay for, three cents a bowl, and they like this best, and it is done for three weeks. They go up there and have full bowls, and I have a long table made before a bench where sometimes they rest, with oil-cloth, and here they eat and are comfortable. Three days soup, three days hot coffee; and I have place where the men can heat what is in their pails.

"But they do such things! They pick out vegetable from soup and throw on the floor. They pour away coffee. They make the place like a home of animals, and when I say, 'Girls, I want much that all should be clean and nice, and that you never waste,' they laugh again. I find that difficult, for what answer can be made to laugh? I go on, but they break bowls and insult the Swiss that make the soup, and tell her I buy dog-meat and such, and she say she will no more of it. Then I call the doctor again and say to them, 'Listen while he tells you what is good to eat.' They were not all so fools, but the fool ones rule, and they listen, but they laugh always. That is American,—to laugh and think everything joke and not see what earnest must be for any good living. I give the coffee-urn to the best girl and tell her to have care of it, but do what we will they think somehow I am silly, and like best to eat their pie and then talk. A small pie at the corner is three cents, and they buy one, sometimes two, and it is sweet and fills and they are content. It is only men that think that will change a habit. I find for the worker always till thought begins they are conservative, and an experiment, a change, is distress to them. So I say, 'Let them do they will. Air is here and that they cannot stop, but for food I will do no more.'

"These all were small things, and as I went on I said, as in the beginning, that for those who did the same work must be the same wage. My men had always ten dollars, and sometimes twelve or fifteen dollars a week; but the best woman had ten dollars, and she had worked five years and knew all. It is a law—unwritten, but still a law—that women shall not have what men earn; and when I say one is good as another, the brother of the woman I make equal with him said first this should never be; and when I said 'It must,' he talk to all the men at noon, and before the looms begin again they come and tell me that if I do so they will work no more. I talk to them all: 'This is a country where men boast always that woman has much honor, but I see not that she has more justice than where there is less honor. Shame on men that will let women work all the hours and as well as they,— yes, many times better,—and then threaten strike if they are paid the same!' But it was all no good. For that time I must yield, because I had much work that was promised; but I said: 'For now I do as you will. With January, that is but a month away, it shall be as I will.'

"Well, I have tried. Many changes have been made, much time lost, much money. I call them to my house in the evening. I talk with them and try to teach them justice, and some are willing, but most not. New men spoil my work, and I lose much profit and take the old ones again. But this, too, is a small thing. My own mind goes on and I see that they should share with me. I read of co-operation, and to me it is truer than profit-sharing. I have seventy men and girls at work. I say they must understand this business. I will try to teach them. Two evenings a week I meet them all and talk and listen to them. One or two feel it plain. For most they say, 'Old B——— wants to get a rise out of us somehow.' At last I see that they are too foolish to understand co-operation, but it may be they will let profit-sharing be a step. Over and over, many times over and over, I tell it all, and in the end some agree, and for a year it does well. But the next year was bad. Silk was high, and my ribbons honest ribbons and profit small; and when they saw how small, they cried that they were cheated and that I kept all for myself. I read them the books. I said, 'Here, you may see with your eyes. This year I make not enough to live if there were not other years in which I saved. I am almost failed. The business might stop, but I will go on for our names' sake.' 'All a dodge,' they said. No words were plain enough to make them know. They even called me cheat and liar, there in the place where I had tried to work for them.

"And so I share profits no more. I give large wage. I never cut down, do the market what it will. But some things are plain. It is not alone oppression and greed from above that do what you call grind the worker. No, I am not alone. There are men like me with a wish for humanity and wiser than I, and alike they are not heard when they speak; alike their wish is naught and their effort vain. It is ignorance that rules. There is no knowledge, no understanding. In my trade and in all trades I know it is the same. A man will not believe a fact, and he will believe that to cheat is all one over him can wish. Even my workers that care for me, a few of them, they laugh no more to my face, but they say: 'Oh, he has notions, that man! He will never get very rich, he has so many notions.' They listen and they think a little. One man said yesterday: 'If this had been put in my head when I was a growing lad it would have straightened many a thing. Why ain't we taught?' And I said to him: 'Jacob, teachers are not taught. There is only one here, one there, that thinks what only it is well to learn,—justice for all the world. I who would do justice am made to wait, but the sin is with you, not with me.'

"So to-day I wait for such time as wisdom may come. My son is one with me in this. He has a plan and soon he will try, and where I failed his more knowledge may do better. But for me, I think that this generation must suffer much, and in pain and want learn, it may be, what is life. To-day it knows not and cares not, save a few. How shall the many be made to know?"

CHAPTER FOURTEENTH.

THE WIDOW MALONEY'S BOARDERS.

TO the old New-Yorker taking his pensive way through streets where only imagination can supply the old landmarks, long ago vanished, there is a conviction that he knows the city foot by foot as it has crept northward; and he repudiates the thought that its growth has ended such possibility, and that many a dark corner is as remote from his or any knowledge save that of its occupants as if in Caffre-land. The newest New-Yorker has small interest in anything but the west side and the space down-town occupied by his store or office.

And so it chances that in spite of occasional series of descriptive articles, in spite of an elaborately written local history and unnumbered novels whose background is the city life and thought, there is little real knowledge, and, save among charitable workers, the police, and adventurous newspaper men, no thought of what life may be lived not a stone's-throw from the great artery of New York, Broadway.

On one point there can be no doubt. Not Africa in its most pestilential and savage form holds surer disease or more determined barbarians than nest together under many a roof within hearing of the rush and roar of the busy streets where men come and go, eager for no knowledge or wisdom under the sun save the knowledge that will make them better bargainers. There comes even a certain impatient distrust of those who persist in unsavory researches and more unsavory details of the results. If there is not distrust; if the easy-going kindliness that is a portion of the American temperament is stirred, it is but for the moment; and when the hand that sought the pocket or the check-book instinctively has presented its gift, interest is over. A fresh sensation wipes out all trace of the transient feeling, and though it may again be roused by judicious effort, how rarely is it that more than the automatic movement toward the pocket results! What might come if for even one hour the impatient giver walked through the dark passages, stood in the foul, dimly lighted rooms and saw what manner of creature New York nourishes in her slums, giving to every child in freest measure that training in all foulness that eye or ear or mind can take in that will fit it in time for the habitation in prison or reformatory on which money is never spared,—who shall say? They are filled by free choice, these nests of all evil. The men and women who herd in them know nothing better; indeed, may have known something even worse. They are Polish Jews,

Bohemians, the lowest order of Italians, content with unending work, the smallest wage, and an order of food that the American, no matter how low he may be brought, can never stomach. Yet they assimilate in one point, being as bent upon getting on as the most determined American, and accepting to this end conditions that seem more those of an Inferno than anything the upper world has known. It is among these people, chiefly Polish Jews and Bohemians, with the inevitable commixture of Irish, that one finds the worst forms of child-labor; children that in happy homes are still counted babies here in these dens beginning at four or five to sew on buttons or pick out threads.

It is not of child-labor and the outrages involved in it that I speak to-day, save indirectly, as it forms part of the mass of evil making up the present industrial system and to be encountered at every turn by the most superficial investigation. It is rather of certain specific conditions, found at many points in tenement-house life, but never in such accumulated degree of vileness at any point save one outside the Fourth Ward. And if the reader, like various recent correspondents, is disposed to believe that I am merely "making up a case," using a little experience and a great deal of imagination, I refer him or her to the forty-third annual report of the New York Association for the Improvement of the Condition of the Poor. There, in detail to a degree impossible here, will be found the official report of the inspector appointed to examine the conditions of life in the building known as "The Big Flat," in Mulberry Street. There are smaller houses that are worse in construction and condition, but there is none controlled by one management where so many are gathered under one roof. The first floor has rooms for fourteen families, the remaining five for sixteen each; and the census of 1880 gave the number of inhabitants as 478, a sufficient number to make up the population of the average village. The formal inspection and the report upon it were made in September, 1886, and the report is now accessible to all who desire information on these phases of city life. It is Mrs. Maloney herself whose methods best give us the heart of the matter, and who, having several callings, is the owner of an experience which appears to hold as much surprise for herself as for the hearer.

"Shure I foind things that interestin' that I'm in no haste to be through wid 'em, an' on for me taste o' purgatory, not hintin' that there mightn't be more 'n a taste," Mrs. Maloney said, on a day in which she unfolded to me her views of life in general, her small gray eyes twinkling, her arms akimbo on her mighty hips, and her cap-border flapping about a face weather-beaten and high-colored to a degree not warranted even by her present profession as apple-woman. Whether whiskey or stale beer is more responsible is unknown. It is only certain that, having submitted with the utmost cheerfulness to the perennial beatings of a husband only half her size, she found consolation in a glass now and then with a sympathizing neighbor and at last in a daily resort to the same friend. There had been a gradual descent from prosperity. Dennis, if small, was wiry and phenomenally strong, and earned steady wages as porter during their first years in the country. But the children, as they grew, went to the bad entirely, living on the earnings of the mother, who washed and scrubbed and slaved, with a heart always full of excuses for the hulking brutes, who came naturally at last to the ends that might have been foretold. Their education had been in the Fourth Ward; they were champion bullies and ruffians of whom the ward still boasts, Mrs. Maloney herself acquiring a certain distinction as the mother of the hardest cases yet sent up from Cherry Street. But if she had no power to save her own, life became easier for whomsoever she elected to guard. Wretched children crept under her wing to escape the beating awaiting them when they had failed to bring home the amount demanded of them. Women, beaten and turned out into the night, fled to her for comfort, and the girl who had lost her place, or to whom worse misfortune had come, told her story to the big-hearted sinner, who nodded and cried and said, "It's the Widdy Maloney that'll see you're not put upon more. Hold on an' be aisy, honey, an' all'll come out the way you'd be havin' it, an' why not?"

It was at this stage of experience that Mrs. Maloney decided to remove to the Big Flat. The last raid of Dennis, the youngest and only boy not housed at the expense of the State, had reduced her belongings to their lowest terms, and she took possession of her new quarters, accompanied only by a rickety table, three chairs, a bed with two old straw mattresses, and some quilts too ragged to give any token of their original characteristics, a stove which owned but one leg,—the rest being supplied by bricks,—and such dishes and other small furniture as could be carried in a basket. But there went with her a girl kicked out by the last man who had temporarily called her his mistress,—a mere child still, who at ten had begun work in a bag-factory passing through various grades of slightly higher employment, till seduced by the floor-walker of the store that it had been her highest ambition to reach. Almost as much her fault as his undoubtedly, her silly head holding but one desire, that for fine clothes and never to work any more, but a woman's heart waking in her when the baby came, and prompting her to harder work and better life than she had ever known. There was no chance of either with the baby, and when at last she farmed out the encumbrance to an old couple in a back building who made this their business, and took a place again in the store, it was relief as well as sorrow that came when the wretched little life was over. But the descent had been a swift one. When what she had called life was quite over, and she sat dumb and despairing in the doorway to which she had been thrust, thinking of the river as the last refuge left, the widow had pushed her before her up the stairs and said,—

"Poor sowl, if there's none to look out for ye, then who but me should do it?"

This was the companion who lay by her side under the ragged quilts, life still refusing to give place to death, though every paroxysm of coughing shortened the conflict.

"She's that patient that the saints themselves—all glory to their blessed names!—couldn't be more so; but I'd not know how to manage if it wasn't for the foot-warmer I call her; that's Angela there, wid eyes that go through you an' the life beaten out of her by the man that called himself her father, an' wasn't at all, at all. It's she that does the kaping of the house, an' sleeps across the foot, an' it's mine they think the two av 'em, else they'd never a let me in, the rules bein', 'no lodgers.' It's not lodgers they are. It's me boarders, full fledged, an' who's a better right than me, though I'd not be sayin' so to the housekeeper that'd need forty pair o' eyes to her two to see what's goin' on under her nose."

The "foot-warmer's" office had ceased for one of them before the month ended, and when the Potter's Field had received the pine coffin followed only by the two watchers, the widow made haste to bring in another candidate for the same position; one upon whom she had kept her eye for a month, certain that worse trouble was on the way than loss of work.

"There was the look on her that manes but the one thing," she said afterward. "There's thim that sthand everything an' niver a word, an' there's thim that turns disperate. She was a disperate wan."

Never had a "disperate wan" better reason. A factory girl almost from babyhood, her apprenticeship having begun at seven, she had left the mill at fourteen, a tall girl older than her years in look and experience. New York was her Mecca, and to New York she came, with a week's wages in her pocket on which to live till work should be found, and neither relative nor friend save a girl who had preceded her by a few months and was now at work in a fringe and gimp factory, earning seven dollars a week and promising the same to the child after a few weeks' training. But seven years in a cotton-mill, if they had given quickness in one direction, had blunted all power in others. The fingers were unskilful and clumsy and her mind too wandering and inattentive to master details, and the place was quickly lost. She entered her name as candidate for the first vacancy in a Grand Street store, and in the mean time went into a coffee and spice mill and became coffee-picker at three dollars a week. This lasted a month or two, but even here there was dissatisfaction with lack of thoroughness, and she was presently discharged. The vacancy had come, and she went at once into the store, her delicate face and pretty eyes commending her to the manager, who lost no time in telling her what impression she could produce if she were better dressed. Weak, irresponsible, hopelessly careless, and past any power to undo these conditions, there was some instinct in the untaught life that put her instantly on the defensive.

"I'm not good for much," she said, "but I'm too good for that. There's nothing you could promise would get you your will and there won't be."

Naturally, as the siege declared itself a hopeless one, the manager found it necessary to fill her place by some more competent hand. There was an interval of waiting in which she pawned almost the last article of clothing remaining that could be dispensed with, and then went into a bakery, where the hours were from seven A. M. to ten P. M., sometimes later. She was awkward at making change, but her gentle manners attracted customers, and the baker himself soon cast a favorable eye upon her, and speedily made the same proposition that had driven her from her last employment. The baker's wife knew the symptoms, and on the same day discharged the girl.

"I don't say it's your fault," she said, "but he's started about you, and it's for your own good I tell you to go. The best thing for you is to go back to your mother, or else take a place with some nice woman that'll keep an eye to you. You'll always be run after. I know your kind, that no man looks at without wanting to fool with 'em. You take my advice and go into a place."

The chance came that night. The mistress of a cheap boarding-house in East Broadway, her patrons chiefly young clerks from Grand and Division Street stores, offered her home and eight dollars a month, and Lizzie, who by this time was frightened and discouraged, accepted on the instant. She was well accustomed to long hours, and she had never minded standing as many of the girls did, her apprenticeship in the mill having made it comparatively easy.

But the drudgery undergone here was beyond anything her life had ever known. Her day began at five and it never ended before eleven. She slept on an old mattress on the kitchen floor, and as her strength failed from the incessant labor, lost all power of protest and accepted each new demand as something against which there could be no revolt. There was abundance of coarse food and thus much advantage, but she had no knowledge that taught her how to make work easier, nor had her mistress any thought of training her. She was a dish-washing machine chiefly, and broke and chipped even the rough ware that formed the table furniture, till the exasperated mistress threatened to turn her off if another piece were destroyed. It was a case of hopeless inaptitude; and when in early spring she sickened, and the physician grudgingly called in declared it a case of typhus brought on by the conditions in which she had lived, she was sent at once to the hospital and left to such fate as might come.

A clean bed, rest, and attendance seemed a heaven to the girl when consciousness came back, and she shrank from any thought of going out again to the fight for existence.

"I don't know what the matter is," she said to the doctor as she mended, "but somehow I ain't fit to make a living. I shall have to go back to the mill, but I said I never would do that."

"You shall go to some training-school and be taught," said the doctor, who had stood looking at her speculatively yet pitifully.

"Ah, but I couldn't learn. Somehow things don't stick to me. I'm not fit to earn a living."

"You're of the same stuff as a good many thousand of your kind," the doctor said under his breath, and turned away with a sigh.

Lizzie went out convalescent, but still weak and uncertain, and took refuge with one of the bakery girls who had half of a dark bedroom in a tenement house near the Big Flat. She looked for work. She answered advertisements, and at last began upon the simplest form of necktie, and in her slow, bungling fashion began to earn again. But she had no strength. She sat at the window and looked over to the Big Flat and watched the swarm that came and went; five hundred people in it, they told her, and half of them drunk at once. It was certain that there were always men lying drunk in the hallways in the midst of ashes and filth that accumulated there almost unchecked. The saloon below was always full; the stale beer dives all along the street full also, above all, at night, when the flaunting street-walkers came out, and fiddles squeaked, and cheap pianos rattled, and songs and shouts were over-topped at moments by the shrieks of beaten women or the oaths and cries of a sudden fight. Slowly it was coming to the girl that this was all the life New York had for her; that if she failed to meet the demand employer after employer had made upon her, she would die in this hole, where neither joy nor hope had any place. Her clothes were in rags. She went hungry and cold, and had grown too stupefied with trouble to plan anything better. At last it was plain to her that death must be best. She said to herself that the river could never tell, and that there would be rest and no more cold or hunger, and it was to the river that she went at night as the Widow Maloney rose before her and said,—

"You'll come home wid me, me dear, an' no wurruds about it."

Lizzie looked at her stupidly. "You'd better not stop me," she said. "I'm no good. I can't earn my living anywhere any more. I don't know how. I'd better be out of the way."

"Shure you'll be enough out o' the way whin you're in the top o' the Big Flat," said Mrs. Maloney. "An' once there we'll see."

Lizzie followed her without a word, but when the stairs were climbed and she sunk panting and ghastly on one of the three chairs, it was quite plain to the widow that more work had begun. That it will very soon end is also quite plain to whoever dares the terrors of the Big Flat, and climbs to the wretched room, which in spite of dirt and foulness within and without is a truer sanctuary than many a better place. The army of incompetents will very shortly be the less by one, but more recruits are in training and New York guarantees an unending supply.

"Shure if there's naught they know how to do," says the widow, "why should one be lookin' to have thim do what they can't. It's one thing I've come to, what with seein' the goings on all me life, but chiefly in the Big Flat, that if childers be not made to learn, whither they like it or not, somethin' that'll keep hands an' head from mischief, there's shmall use in laws an' less in muddlin' about 'em when they're most done with livin' at all, at all. But that's a thing that's beyond me or the likes o' me, an' I'm only wonderin' a thrifle like an' puttin' the question to meself a bit, 'What would you be doin', Widdy Maloney, if the doin' risted on you an' no other?'"

CHAPTER FIFTEENTH.

AMONG THE SHOP-GIRLS.

WHY this army of women, many thousand strong, is standing behind counters, over-worked and underpaid, the average duration of life among them as a class lessening every year, is a question with which we can at present deal only indirectly. It is sufficient to state that the retail stores of wellnigh every order, though chiefly the dry-goods retail trade, have found their quickness and aptness to learn, the honesty and general faithfulness of women, and their cheapness essentials in their work; and that this combination of qualities—cheapness dominating all—has given them permanent place in the modern system of trade. A tour among many of the larger establishments confirmed the statement made by employers in smaller ones, the summary being given in the words of a manager of one of the largest retail houses to be found in the United States.

"We don't want men," he said. "We wouldn't have them even if they came at the same price. Of course cheapness has something to do with it, and will have, but for my part give me a woman to deal with every time. Now there's an illustration over at that hat-counter. We were short of hands to-day, and I had to send for three girls that had applied for places, but were green—didn't know the business. It didn't take them ten minutes to get the hang of doing things, and there they are, and you'd never know which was old and which was new hand. Of course they don't know all about qualities and so on, but the head of the department looks out for that. No, give me women every time. I've been a manager thirteen years, and we never had but four dishonest girls, and we've had to discharge over forty boys in the same time. Boys smoke and lose at cards, and do a hundred things that women don't, and they get worse instead of better. I go in for women."

"How good is their chance of promotion?"

"We never lose sight of a woman that shows any business capacity, but of course that's only as a rule in heads of departments. A saleswoman gets about the same right along. Two thirds of the girls here are public-school girls and live at home. You see that makes things pretty easy, for the family pool their earnings and they dress well and live well. We don't take from the poorer class at all. These girls earn from four and a half to eight dollars a week. A few get ten dollars, and they're not likely to do better than that.

Forty dollars a month is a fortune to a woman. A man must have his little fling, you know. Women manage better."

"If they are really worth so much to you, why can't you give better pay? What chance has a girl to save anything, unless she lives at home?"

"We give as high pay as anybody, and we don't give more because for every girl here there are a dozen waiting to take her place. As to saving, she doesn't want to save. There isn't a girl here that doesn't expect to marry before long, and she puts what she makes on her back, because a fellow naturally goes for the best-looking and the best-dressed girl. That's the woman question as I've figured it out, and you'll find it the same everywhere."

Practically he was right, for the report, though varying slightly, summed up as substantially the same. Descending a grade, it was found that even in the second and third rate stores the system of fines for any damage soon taught the girls carefulness, and that while a few were discharged for hopeless incompetency, the majority served faithfully and well.

"I dare say they're put upon," said the manager of one of the cheaper establishments. "They're sassy enough, a good many of them, and some of the better ones suffer for their goings-on. But they ain't a bad set—not half; and these women that come in complaining that they ain't well-treated, nine times out of ten it's their own airs that brought it on. It's a shop-girl's interest to behave herself and satisfy customers, and she's more apt to do it than not, according to my experience."

"They'd drive a man clean out of his mind," said another. "The tricks of girls are beyond telling. If it wasn't for fines there wouldn't one in twenty be here on time, and the same way with a dozen other things. But they learn quick, and they turn in anywhere where they're wanted. They make the best kind of clerks, after all."

"Do you give them extra pay for over-hours during the busy season?"

"Not much! We keep them on, most of them, right through the dull one. Why shouldn't they balance things for us when the busy time comes? Turn about's fair play."

A girl who had been sent into the office for some purpose shook her head slightly as she heard the words, and it was this girl who, a day or two later, gave her view of the situation. The talk went on in the pretty, home-like parlors of a small "Home" on the west side, where rules are few and the atmosphere of the place so cheery that while it is intended only for those out of work, it is constantly besieged with requests to enlarge its borders and make room for more. Half a dozen other girls were near: three from other stores, one from a shirt factory, one an artificial-flower-maker who had been a shop-girl.

"When I began," said the first, "father was alive, and I used what I earned just for dressing myself. We were up at Morrisania, and I came down every day. I was in the worsted and fancy department at D——'s, and I had such a good eye for matching and choosing that they seemed to think everything of me. But then father fell sick. He was a painter, and had painter's colic awfully and at last paralysis. Then he died finally and left mother and me, and she's in slow consumption and can't do much. I earned seven dollars a week because I'd learned fancy work and did some things evenings for the store, and we should have got along very well. We'd had to move out a little farther, to the place mother was born in, because rent was cheaper and she could never stand the city. But this is the way it worked. I have to be at the store at eight o'clock. The train that leaves home at seven gets me to the store two minutes after eight, but though I've explained this to the manager he says I've got to be at the store at eight, and so, summer and winter, I have to take the train at half-past six and wait till doors are open. It's the same way at night. The store closes at six, and if I could leave then I could catch an express train that would get me home at seven. The rules are that I must stop five minutes to help the girls cover up the goods, and that just hinders my getting the train till after seven, so that I am not home till eight."

I looked at the girl more attentively. She was colorless and emaciated, and, when not excited by speaking, languid and heavy.

"Are you sure that you have explained the thing clearly so that the manager understands?" I asked.

"More than once," the girl answered, "but he said I should be fined if I were not there at eight. Then I told him that the girls at my counter would be glad to cover up my goods, and if he would only let me go at six it would give me a little more time for mother. I sit up late anyway to do things she can't, for we live in two rooms and I sew and do a good many things after I go home."

Inquiry a day or two later showed that her story was true in every detail and also that she was a valuable assistant, one of the best among a hundred or so employed. The firm gives largely to charitable objects, and pays promptly, and at rates which, if low, are no lower than usual; but they continue to exact this seven minutes' service from one whose faithfulness might seem to have earned exemption from a purely arbitrary rule—in such a case mere tyranny. The girl had offered to give up her lunch hour, but the manager refused; and she dared not speak again for fear of losing her place.

"After all, she's better off than I am or lots of others," said one who sat near her. "I'm down in the basement at M——'s, and forty others like me, and about forty little girls. There's gas and electric light both, but there isn't a breath of air, and it's so hot that after an hour or two your head feels baked and your eyes as if they would fall out. The dull season—that's from spring to fall—lasts six months, and then we work nine and a half hours and Saturdays thirteen. The other six months we work eleven hours, and holiday time till ten and eleven. I'm strong. I'm an old hand and somehow stand things, but I've a cousin at the ribbon counter, the very best girl in the world, I do believe. She always makes the best of things, but this year it did seem as if the whole town was at that counter. They stood four and five deep. She was penned in with the other girls, a dozen or two, with drawers and cases behind and counter in front, and there she stood from eight in the morning till ten at night, with half an hour off for dinner and for supper. She could have got through even that, but you see there has to be steady passing in that narrow space, and she was knocked and pushed, first by one and then by another, till she was sore all over; and at last down she dropped right there, not fainting, but sort of gone, and the doctor says she's most dead and can't go back, he doesn't know when. Down there in the basement the girls have to put on blue glasses, the glare is so dreadful, but they don't like to have us. The only comfort is you're with a lot and don't feel lonesome. I can't bear to do anything alone, no matter what it is."

A girl with clear dark eyes and a face that might have been almost beautiful but for its haggard, worn-out expression, turned from the table where she had been writing and smiled as she looked at the last speaker.

"That is because you happen to be made that way," she said. "I am always happier when I can be alone a good deal, but of course that's never possible, or almost never. I shall want the first thousand years of my heaven quite to myself, just for pure rest and a chance to think."

"I don't know anything about heaven," the last speaker said hastily, "but I'm sure I hope there's purgatory at least for some of the people I've had to submit to. I think a woman manager is worse than a man. I've never had trouble anywhere and always stay right on, but I've wanted to knock some of the managers down, and it ought to have been done. Just take the new superintendent. We loved the old one, but this one came in when she died, and one of the first things she did was to discharge one of the old girls because she didn't smile enough. Good reason why. She'd lost her mother the week before and wasn't likely to feel much like smiling. And then she went inside the counters and pitched out all the old shoes the girls had there to make it easier to stand. It 'most kills you to stand all day in new shoes, but Miss T—— pitched them all out and said she wasn't going to have the store turned into an old-clothes shop."

"Well, it's better than lots of them, no matter what she does," said another. "I was at H———'s for six months, and there you have to ask a man for leave every time it is necessary to go upstairs, and half the time he would look and laugh with the other clerks. I'd rather be where there are all women. They're hard on you sometimes, but they don't use foul language and insult you when you can't help yourself."

This last complaint has proved for many stores a perfectly well-founded one. Wash-rooms and other conveniences have been for common use, and many sensitive and shrinking girls have brought on severe illnesses arising solely from dread of running this gantlet.

Here and there the conditions of this form of labor are of the best, but as a whole the saleswoman suffers not only from long-continued standing, but from bad air, ventilation having no place in the construction of the ordinary store. Separate dressing-rooms are a necessity, yet are only occasionally found, the system demanding that no outlay shall be made when it is possible to avoid it. Overheating and overcrowding, hastily eaten and improper food, are all causes of the weakness and anæmic condition so perceptible among shop and factory workers, these being divided into many classes. For a large proportion it can be said that they are tolerably educated, so far as our public-school system can be said to educate, and are hard-working, self-sacrificing, patient girls who have the American knack of dressing well on small outlay, and who have tastes and aspirations far beyond any means of gratifying them. For such girls the working-women's guilds and the Friendly societies—these last of English origin—have proved of inestimable service, giving them the opportunities long denied. In such guilds many of them receive the first real training of eye and hand and mind, learn what they can best do, and often develop a practical ability for larger and better work. Even in the lowest order filling the cheaper stores there is always a proportion eager to learn. But here, as in all ordinary methods of learning, the market is overstocked, and even the best-trained girl may sometimes fail of employment. Now and then one turns toward household service, but the mass prefer any cut in wages and any form of privation to what they regard as almost a final degradation. A multitude of their views on this point are recorded and will in time find place.

In the mean time a minute examination of the causes that determine their choice and of the conditions surrounding it as a whole go to prove the justice of the conviction that penetrates the student of social problems. Again, the shop-girl as a class demonstrates the fact that not with her but with the class above her, through accident of birth or fortune, lies the real responsibility for the follies over which we make moan. The cheaper daily papers record in fullest detail the doings of that fashionable world toward which many a weak girl or woman looks with unspeakable longing; and the weekly "story papers" feed the flame with unending details of the rich marriage that lifted the poor girl into the luxury which stands to her empty mind as the sole thing to be desired in earth or heaven. She knows far better what constitutes the life of the rich than the rich ever know of the life of the poor. From her post behind the counter the shop-girl examines every detail of costume, every air and grace of these women whom she despises, even when longing most to be one of them. She imitates where she can, and her cheap shoe has its French heel, her neck its tin dog-collar. Gilt rings and bracelets and bangles, frizzes and bangs and cheap trimmings of every order, swallow up her earnings. The imitation is often more effective than the real, and the girl knows it. She aspires to a "manicure" set, to an opera-glass, to anything that will simulate the life daily more passionately desired; and it is small wonder that when sudden temptation comes and the door opens into that land where luxury is at least nearer, she falls an easy victim. The class in which she finally takes rank is seldom recruited from sources that would seem most fruitful. The sewing-woman, the average factory worker, is devitalized to such an extent that even ambition dies and the brain barely responds to even the allurements of the weekly story paper. It is the class but a grade removed, to whom no training has come from which strength or simplicity or any virtue of honest living could grow, that makes the army of women who have chosen degradation.

A woman, herself a worker, but large-brained and large-hearted beyond the common endowment, wrote recently of the dangers put in the way of the average shop or factory girl, imploring happy women living at ease to adopt simpler forms, or at least to ask what form of living went on below them. She wrote:—

"It may be urged that ignorant and inexperienced as these workers are, they see only the bubbles and the froth, the superficial glitter and exuberant overflow of passing styles and social pleasures, and miss much, if not all, of the earnestness, the virtue, the charity, and the refinement which may belong to those they imitate, but with whom they seldom come in contact. This is the very point and purpose of this paper, to remonstrate against the injustice done to the women of wealth and leisure by their own carelessness and indifference, and to urge them to come down to those who cannot come up to them, to study them with as keen an interest as they themselves are studied,—to know how that other half lives."

"To know how that other half lives." That is the demand made upon woman and man alike. Once at least put yourselves in the worker's place, if it be but for half an hour, and think her thought and live her starved and dreary life. Then ask what work must be done to alter conditions, to kill false ideals, and vow that no day on earth shall pass that has not held some effort, in word or deed, to make true living more possible for every child of man. No mission, no guild, no sermon, has or can have power alone. Only in the determined effort of the individual, in individual understanding and renunciation forever of what has been selfish and mean and base, can humanity know redemption and walk at last side by side in that path where he who journeys alone finds no entrance, nor can win it till self has dropped away, and knowledge come that forever we are our brothers' keepers.

CHAPTER SIXTEENTH.

TWO HOSPITAL BEDS.

WHY and how the money-getting spirit has become the ruler of American life and thought no analyzer of social conditions has yet made plain. That New York might be monopolist in this respect could well be conceived, for the Dutch were traders by birthright and New Amsterdam arose to this one end. But why the Puritan colony, whose first act before even the tree stumps were brown in their corn-fields was the founding of a college, and whose corner-stone rested on a book,—why these people should have come to represent a spirit of bargaining and an aptitude for getting on unmatched by the keenest-witted Dutchman hath no man yet told us.

The sharpest business men of the present are chiefly "Yankees;" and if "Jew" and "a hard bargain" are counted synonymes, "New-Englander" has equal claim to the place. The birthplace and home of all reform, New England is the home also of a greed born of hard conditions and developing a keenness unequalled by that of any other bargainer on earth. The Italian, the Greek, the Turk, find a certain æsthetic satisfaction in bargaining and do it methodically, but always picturesquely and with a relish unaffected by defeat; but with the Yankee it is a passionate, absorbing desire, sharpening every line of the face and felt even in the turn of the head or shoulders, and in every line of the eager, restless figure. Success assured softens and modifies these tendencies. Defeat aggravates them. One meets many a man for whom it is plain that the beginning of life held unlimited faith that the great city meant a fortune, the sanguine conviction passing gradually into the interrogative form. The fortune is still there. Thus far the conviction holds good, but his share in it has become more and more problematical. The flying and elusive shadow still holds for him the only real substance, but his hands have had no power to grasp or detain, and the most dogged determination gives way at last to the sense of hopeless failure. For this type may be the ending as cheap clerk or bookkeeper, with furtive attempts at speculation when a few dollars have been saved, or a retreat toward that remote West which has hidden effectually so many baffled and defeated lives. There may also come another ending, and the feverish, scheming soul lose its hold on the body, which has meant to it merely a means of getting and increasing money.

It is this latter fate that came to a man who would have no place in this record save for the fact that his last querulous and still-questioning days were lived side by side with a man who had also sought money, and having found it had chosen for it certain experimental uses by means of which siphon he was presently drained dry. For him also had been many defeats. A hospital ward held them both, and the two beds were side by side, the one representing a patience that never failed, yet something more than patience. For the face of this man bore no token of defeat. It was rather triumph that looked at moments from the clear eyes that had also an almost divine pity as they turned toward the neighbor who poured out his story between paroxysms of coughing, and having told it once, proceeded to tell it again, his sole and final satisfaction in life being the arraignment of all living. The visitor who came into the ward was pinned on the instant, the fiery eyes demanding the hearing which was the last gift time held for him. It was a common story often told, this slow, inevitable descent into poverty. Its force lay in the condensed fury of the speaker, who looked on the men he had known as sworn conspirators against him, and cursed them in their going out and coming in with a relish that no argument could affect. What his neighbor might have to tell was a matter of the purest indifference. It was impossible even to ask his story; and it remained impossible until a day when arraignment was cut short and the disappointed, bitter soul passed on to such conditions as it had made for itself.

"You've got the best of me. They all do," he said in dying, with a last turn of the sombre eyes toward his neighbor. "You ought to have gone first by a week, and there you are. But this time I guess it's just as well. I don't seem to want to fight any longer, and I'm glad I'm done. It's your turn next. Good—"

The words had come with gasps between and long pauses. Here they stopped once for all. Good had found him; the only good for the child of earth, who, having failed to learn his lesson here, must try a larger school with a different system of training. The empty bed was not filled at once. A screen shut it off. There was time now to hear other words than the passionate railings that had monopolized all time. The sick man mended a little, and in one of the days in which speech was easier gave this record of his forty years:—

"It's a fact, I believe, that the sons of reformers seldom walk in the same track. My father was one of the old Abolitionists, and an honest one, ready to give money when he could and any kind of work when he couldn't. It was a great cause. I cried over the negroes down South and went without sugar a year or so, and learned to knit so that I could knit some stockings for the small slaves my own size. But by the time I was eight years old it was plain enough to me that there were other kinds of slavery quite as bad, and that my own mother wore as heavy bonds as any of them. She was a farmer's wife, and from year's end to year's end she toiled and worked. She never had a cent of her own, for the butter money was consecrated to the cause, and she gave it gladly. My father had no particular intention to be unkind. He was simply like a good two-thirds of the farmers I have known,—much more careful of his animals than of his wife. A woman was so much cooking and cleaning and butter-making force, and child-bearing an incident demanding as little notice as possible. It is because of that theory that I am five inches shorter than any of our tribe. My mother was a tall, slender woman, with a springy step and eyes as clear as a brook. I see them sometimes as I lie here at night.

"I said to myself when I was ten that I'd have things easier for her before she died. I said it straight ahead while I was working my way up in the village store, for I would not farm, and when she died I said it to her in the last hour I ever heard her voice: 'What I couldn't do for you, mother, I'll do for all women as long as I am on the earth.'

"I was eighteen then, and whichever way I turned some woman was having a hard time, and some brute was making it for her. I knew it was partly their own fault for not teaching their boys how to be unselfish and decent, but custom and tradition, the law and the prophets, were all against them. I watched it all I could, but I was deep in trying to get ahead and I did. Somehow, in spite of my dreams and my fancies, there was a money-making streak in me. It's a lost vein. You may search as you will and find no trace, but it was there once and gave good returns. I left the village at twenty-one and went to Philadelphia, and the small savings I took with me from my clerking soon began to roll up. I had the chance to go into a soap-factory; a queer change, but the old Quaker who owned it knew my father and wanted to do me a good turn, and by the time I had got the hang of it all I was junior partner and settled for life if I liked.

"Well, here it was again. This man was honest and clean. He meant to do fairly by all mankind, and he tried to. He had some secrets in his methods that made his soap the best in the market. The chief secret was honest ingredients, but it was famous. If you've ever been in a soap-factory you know what it is like. Every pound of it was wrapped in paper as fast as it cooled, and the cooling and cutting room was filled with girls who did the work. They were not the best order of girls. The wages a week were from three to five dollars, and they were at it from seven A. M. to six P. M. There was a good woman in the office,—a woman with a head as well as a heart,—and she did the directing and disciplining. It was no joke to keep peace if the cooling delayed and the creatures began squabbling together, but she managed it, and by night they were always meek enough. You're likely to be meek when you've carried soap ten pounds at a time ten hours a day, from the cutting table to the cooling table, across floors as slippery as glass or glare ice. They picked it up as it cooled, wrapped it in paper, and had it in boxes, five pounds to the minute, three hundred pounds an hour. The caustic soda in it first turned their nails orange-color and then it ate off their finger tips till they bled. They could not wear gloves, for that would have interfered with the packing.

"Now and then one cried, but only seldom. They were big, hearty girls. They had to be to do that work, but my heart ached for them as they filed out at night, so worn that there was no life left for anything but to get home and into bed. Very few stayed on. The smart ones graduated into something better. The stupid ones fell back and tried something easier. But as I watched them and it came over me how untrained and helpless they were, and how every chance of learning was cut off by the long labor and the dead weariness, I said to myself that we owed them something: shorter hours; better wages; some sort of share in the money we were making. Friend Peter shook his head when I began to hint these things. 'They fare well enough,' he said. 'Thee must not get socialistic notions in thy head.' 'I know nothing about socialism,' I said. 'All I want is justice, and thee wants it too. Thee has cried out for it for the black brother and sister; why not for the white?'

"'Thee is talking folly,' he said and would make no other answer.

"It all weighed on me. Here was the money rolling in, or so it seemed to me. We did make it in a sure, comfortable fashion. I was well off at twenty-five, and better off every month; and I said to myself, the money would have a curse on it if those who helped to earn it had no share. I talked to the men in the boiling department. It takes brains to be a good soap-maker. We kept to the old ways, simply because what they call improvement in soap-making, like many another improvement, has been the cheapening the product by the addition of various articles that lower the quality. Experience has to teach. Theoretical knowledge isn't much use save as foundation. A man must use eyes and tongue, and watch for the critical moment in the finishing like a lynx.

"Well, I beat my head against that wall of obstinacy till head and heart were sore. It was enough to the old Quaker that he paid promptly and did honest work; and when I told him at last that his gains were as fraudulent as if he cheated deliberately, he said, 'Then thee need share them no longer. Go thy way for a hot-headed fool.'

"I went. There was an opening in New York, and I had every detail at my fingers' ends. I went in with a man a little older, who seemed to think as I did, and who did, till I made practical application of my theories. I had studied everything to be had on the subject. I had mastered a language or two in my evenings, for I lived like a hermit; but now I began to talk with every business man, and try to understand why competition was inevitable. I was in no haste. I admitted that men must be trained to co-operate, but I said, 'We shall never learn by waiting. We must learn by trying.' I tried to bring in other soap-makers, and one or two listened; but most of them were using the cheap methods,—increasing the quantity and lowering the quality. Some of the men had come on to me from Philadelphia, and were bound to stay, but it was hard on them. They had to go into tenement-houses, for there were no homes for them such as building associations in Philadelphia make possible for every workman. But I took a house and divided it up and made it comfortable, and I lived on the lower floor myself, so that kept them contented. I fitted up a room for a reading-room, and twice a week had talks; not lectures, but talks where every man had a chance to speak five minutes if he would, and to ask questions. I coaxed the women to come. I wanted them to understand, and two or three took hold. I made a decent place for them to eat their dinners, and put these women in charge. I put in an oil-stove and a table and seats, and gave them coffee and tea at two cents a cup, and tried to have them care for the place. That has been done over and over by many an employer who pities his workers; and nine times out of ten the same result follows. The animal crops out. They were rough girls at any time, yet, taken one by one, behaved well enough. But I've seen boys and girls at a donation party throw cheese and what not on the carpet and rub it in deliberately, and I don't know that one need wonder that lunch-rooms in store or factory turn into pig-pens, and the few decent ones can make no headway.

"I spoke out to them all, but it was no more than the wind blowing, and at last even I gave it up. There was no conscience in them to touch. They wanted shorter hours and more money, when they had got to the point of seeing that I was trying to help, but they had no notion of helping back. With my men it worked, and they talked down the women sometimes. But when a bad year came,—for soap has its ups and downs like everything else,—most of them struck, and the wise ones could make no headway. 'It's a losing game,' my partner said; 'if you want to go on you must go on alone.'

"I did go on alone. He left and took his capital with him. The best men stayed with me and swore to take their chances. The soap was good, and I made a hit in one or two fancy kinds, but I could not compete with men who used mean material and turned out something that looked as well at half the price. My money melted away, and a fire—set, they told me, by a man I had discharged for long-continued dishonesty—finished me. I had the name of stirring up strife for the manufacturers, because I tried to teach my workers the principle of co-operation, and begged for it where I could. It hurt my business standing. Men felt that I must be a fool. I had worked for it with such absorption that I had had little time for any joy of life. I had neither wife nor child, though I longed for both. I would not have ease and happiness alone. I wanted it for my fellows. To-day it might be. Ten years ago it only the thought of a dreamer, and I made no headway.

"The fire left me stranded. I went in as superintendent of some new works, but went out in a month, for I could not consent to cheat, and fraud was in every pound sent out. I tried one place and another with the same result. Competition makes honesty impossible. A man would admit it to me without hesitation, but would end: 'There's no other way. Don't be a fool. You can't stand out against a system.'

"'I will stand out if it starves me,' I said. 'I will not sell my soul for any man's hire. The time is coming when this rottenness must end. Make one more to fight it now.'

"Men looked at me pitifully. 'I was throwing away chances,' they said. 'Why wouldn't I hear reason? We were in the world, not in Utopia.'

"'We are in the hell we have made for all mankind,' I said. 'The only real world is the world which is founded on truth and justice. Everything else falls away.'

"Everything else has fallen away. I was never strong, and a year ago I was knocked down in a scrimmage. Some bullies from one of the factories set on my men—mine no longer, but still preaching my doctrine. Somehow I was kicked in the chest and a rib broken, and this saved me probably from being sent up as a disturber of the peace. The right lung was wounded, and consumption came naturally. They nursed me—Tom's wife and sister, good souls—till I refused to burden them any longer and came here in spite of them. It has been a sharp fight. I seem to have failed; yet the way is easier for the next. Co-operation will come. It must come. It is the law of life. It is the only path out of this jungle in which we wander and struggle and die. But there must be training. There must be better understanding. I would give a thousand lives joyfully if only I could make men and women who sit at ease know the sorrow of the poor. It is their ignorance that is their curse. Teach them; study them. Care as much for the outcast at home as for the heathen abroad. And, oh, if you can make anybody listen, beg them for Christ's sake, for their own sake, to hearken and to help! Beg them to study; not to say with no knowledge that help is impossible, but to study, to think, and then to work with their might. It is my last word,—a poor word that can reach none, it may be, any more, and yet, who knows what wind of the Lord may bear it on, what ground may be waiting for the seed? I shall see it, but not now. I shall behold it, and it will be nigh, in that place to which I go. Work for it; die for it if need be; for man's hope, man's life, if ever he knows true life, has no other foundation."

CHAPTER SEVENTEENTH.

CHILD-WORKERS IN NEW YORK.

POLITICAL economists in general, with the additional number of those who for one purpose and another turn over statistics of labor, nodded approvingly as they gazed upon the figures of the last general census for the State of New York, which showed that among the myriad of workers in factory and other occupations, but twenty-four thousand children were included.

"Fifty-six million and more inhabitants, and all faring so well that only one fortieth part of one of these millions is employed too early in this Empire State. Civilization could hardly do more. See how America leads among all civilized countries as the protector of the feeble, the guarantee of strength for the weakest. No other country guards its children so well. There have been errors, of course; such enlightenment is not reached at a bound; but the last Legislature made further ones impossible, for it fixed the minimum limit at which a child may be employed in factories at thirteen years of age. By thirteen a child isn't likely to be stunted or hurt by overwork. We protect all classes and the weakest most."

Thus the political economist who stops at figures and considers any further dealing with the question unnecessary. And if the law were of stringent application; if parents told the truth as to age, and if the two inspectors who are supposed to suffice for the thousands of factories in the State of New York were multiplied by fifty, there might be some chance of carrying out the provisions of this law. As it is, it is a mere form of words, evaded daily; a bit of legislation which, like much else bearing with it apparent benefit, proves when analyzed to be not much more than sham. The law applies to factories only. It does not touch mercantile establishments or trades that are carried on in tenement-houses, and it is with these two latter forms of labor that we deal to-day. In factory labor in the city of New York nine thousand children under twelve years of age are doing their part toward swelling the accumulation of wealth, each adding their tiny contribution to the great stream of what we call the prosperity of the nineteenth century. Thus far their share in the trades we have considered has been ignored. Let us see in what fashion they make part of the system.

For a large proportion of the women visited, among whom all forms of the clothing industry were the occupation, children under ten, and more often from four to eight, were valuable assistants. In a small room on Hester Street, a woman on work on overalls—for the making of which she received one dollar a dozen—said:—

"I couldn't do as well if it wasn't for Jinny and Mame there. Mame has learned to sew on buttons first-rate, and Jinny is doing almost as well. I'm alone to-day, but most days three of us sew together here, and Jinny keeps right along. We'll do better yet when Mame gets a bit older."

As she spoke the door opened and a woman with an enormous bundle of overalls entered and sat down on the nearest chair with a gasp.

"Them stairs is killin'," she said. "It's lucky I've not to climb 'em often."

Something crept forward as the bundle slid to the floor, and busied itself with the string that bound it.

"Here you, Jinny," said the woman, "don't you be foolin'. What do you want anyhow?"

The something shook back a mat of thick hair and rose to its feet,—a tiny child who in size seemed no more than three, but whose countenance indicated the experience of three hundred.

"It's the string I want," the small voice said. "Me an' Mame was goin' to play with it."

"There's small time for play," said the mother; "there'll be two pair more in a minute or two, an' you're to see how Mame does one an' do it good too, or I'll find out why not."

Mame had come forward and stood holding to the one thin garment which but partly covered Jinny's little bones. She too looked out from a wild thatch of black hair, and with the same expression of deep experience, the pallid, hungry little faces lighting suddenly as some cheap cakes were produced. Both of them sat down on the floor and ate their portion silently.

"Mame's seven and Jinny's going on six," said the mother, "but Jinny's the smartest. She could sew on buttons when she wasn't but much over four. I had five then, but the Lord's took 'em all but these two. I couldn't get on if it wasn't for Mame."

Mame looked up but said no word, and as I left the room settled herself with her back against the wall, Jinny at her side, laying the coveted string near at hand for use if any minute for play arrived. In the next room, half-lighted like the last, and if possible even dirtier, a Jewish tailor sat at work on a coat, and by him on the floor a child of five picking threads from another.

"Netta is good help," he said after a word or two. "So fast as I finish, she pick all the threads. She care not to go away—she stay by me always to help."

"Is she the only one?"

"But one that sells papers. Last year is five, but mother and dree are gone with fever. It is many that die. What will you? It is the will of God."

On the floor below two children of seven and eight were found also sewing on buttons—in this case for four women who had their machines in one room and were making the cheapest order of corset-cover, for which they received fifty cents a dozen, each one having five buttons. It could not be called oppressive work, yet the children were held there to be ready for each one completed, and sat as such children most often do, silent and half asleep waiting for the next demand.

"It's hard on 'em," one of the women said. "We work till ten and sometimes later, but then they sleep between and we can't; and they get the change of running out for a loaf of bread or whatever's wanted, and we don't stir from the machine from morning till night. I've got two o' me own, but they're out peddling matches."

On the lower floor back of the small grocery in which the people of the house bought their food supply,—wilted or half-decayed vegetables, meat of the cheapest order, broken eggs and stale fish,—a tailor and two helpers were at work. A girl of nine or ten sat among them and picked threads or sewed on buttons as needed; a haggard, wretched-looking child who did not look up as the door opened. A woman who had come down the stairs behind me stopped a moment, and as I passed out said:—

"If there was a law for him I'd have him up. It's his own sister's child, and he workin' her ten hours a day an' many a day into the night, an' she with an open sore on her neck, an' crying out many's the time when she draws out a long needleful an' so gives it a jerk. She's sewed on millions of buttons, that child has, an' she but a little past ten. May there be a hot place waitin' for him!"

A block or two beyond, the house entered proved to be given over chiefly to cigar-making. It is to this trade that women and girls turn during the dull season, and one finds in it representatives from every trade in which women are engaged. The sewing-women employed in suit and clothing manufactories during the busy season have no resource save this, and thus prices are kept down and the regular cigar-makers constantly reinforced by the irregular. In the present case it was chiefly with regular makers that the house was filled, one room a little less than twelve by fourteen feet holding a family of seven persons, three of them children under ten, all girls.

Tobacco lay in piles on the floor and under the long table at one end where the cigars were rolled, its rank smell dominating that from the sinks and from the general filth, not only of this room but of the house as a whole. Two of the children sat on the floor stripping the leaves, and another on a small stool. A girl of twenty sat near them, and all alike had sores on lips and cheeks and on the hands. Children from five or six years up can be taught to strip and thus add to the week's income, which is far less for the tenement-house manufacture than for regular factory work, the latter averaging from eight to twelve dollars a week. But the work if done at home can be made to include the entire family, and some four thousand women are engaged in it, an almost equal but unregistered number of young children sharing it with them. As in sewing, a number of women often club together, using one room, and in such case their babies crawl about in the filth on the wet floors, playing with the damp tobacco and breathing the poison with which the room is saturated.

Here, as in tobacco factories, women and girls of every age become speedily the victims of nervous and hysterical complaints, the direct result of nicotine poisoning; while succeeding these come consumption and throat diseases resulting from the dust. Canker is one of the most frequent difficulties, and sores of many orders, the trade involving more dangers than any that can be chosen. Yet because an entire family can find occupation in it, with no necessity for leaving home, it is often preferred to easier employment. It is the children who suffer most, growth being stunted, nervous disease developed and ending often in St. Vitus's dance, and skin diseases of every order being the rule, the causes being not only tobacco, but the filth in which they live.

It is doubtful if the most inveterate smoker would feel much relish for the cigar manufactured under such conditions; yet hundreds of thousands go out yearly from these houses, bearing in every leaf the poison of their preparation. In this one house nearly thirty children of all ages and sizes, babies predominating, rolled in the tobacco which covered the floor and was piled in every direction; and of these children under ten thirteen were strippers and did their day's work of ten hours and more. Physical degeneration in its worst forms becomes inevitable. Even the factory child-worker fares better, for in the factory there is exercise and the going to and from work, while in the tenement-house cigar-making the worn-out little creatures crawl to the bed, often only a pile of rags in the corner, or lie down on a heap of the tobacco itself, breathing this poison day and night uninterruptedly. Vices of every order flourish in such air, and morality in this trade is at lowest ebb. Nervous excitement is so intense that necessarily nothing but immorality can result, and the child of eight or ten is as gross and confirmed an offender as the full-grown man or woman. Diligent search discovers few exceptions to this rule, and the whole matter has reached a stage where legislative interference is absolutely indispensable. Only in forbidding tenement-house manufacture absolutely can there be any safety for either consumer or producer.

Following in the same line of inquiry I take here the facts furnished to Professor Adler by a lady physician whose work has long lain among the poor. During the eighteen months prior to February 1, 1886, she found among the people with whom she came in contact five hundred and thirty-five children under twelve years old,—most of them between ten and twelve,—who either worked in shops or stores or helped their mothers in some kind of work at home. Of these five hundred and thirty-five children but sixty were healthy. In one family a child at three years old had infantile paralysis, easily curable. The mother had no time to attend to it. At five years old the child was taught to sew buttons on trousers. She is now at thirteen a hopeless cripple; but she finishes a dozen pair of trousers a day, and her family are thus twenty cents the richer. In another family she found twin girls four and a half years old sewing on buttons from six in the morning till ten at night; and near them was a family of three,—a woman who did the same work and whose old father of eighty and little girl of six were her co-workers.

There is a compulsory education law, but it demands only fourteen weeks of the year, and the poorer class work from early morning till eight A. M. and after school hours from four till late in the night. With such energy as is left they take their fourteen weeks of education, but even in these many methods of evasion are practised. It is easy to swear that the child is over fourteen, but small of its age, and this is constantly done. It is sometimes done deliberately by thinking workmen, who deny that the common school as it at present exists can give any training that they desire for their children, or that it will ever do so till manual training forms part of the course. But for most it is not intelligent dissatisfaction, but the absorbing press of getting a living that compels the employment of child-labor, and thus brings physical and moral degeneration, not only for this generation but for many to come. It is not alone the nine thousand in factories that we must deal with, but many hundred thousands uncounted and unrecognized, the same spirit dominating all.

In one of the better class of tenement-houses a woman, a polisher in a jewelry manufactory, said the other day:—

"I'm willing to work hard, I don't care how hard; but it's awful to me to see my little boy and the way he goes on. He's a cash-boy at D——'s, and they don't pay by the week, they pay by checks, so every cash-boy is on the keen jump after a call. They're so worried and anxious and afraid they won't get enough; and Johnny cries and says, 'O mamma, I do try, but there's one boy that always gets ahead of me.' I think it's an awful system, even if it does make them smart."

An awful system, yet in its ranks march more and more thousands every year. It would seem as if every force in modern civilization bent toward this one end of money-getting, and the child of days and the old man of years alike shared the passion and ran the same mad race. It is the passion itself that has outgrown all bounds and that faces us to-day,—the modern Medusa on which he who looks has no more heart of flesh and blood but forever heart of stone, insensible to any sorrow, unmoved by any cry of child or woman. It is with this shape that the battle must be, and no man has yet told us its issue. Nay, save here and there one, who counts that battle is needed, or sees the shadow of the terror walking not only in darkness but before all men's eyes, who is there that has not chosen blindness and will not hear the voice that pleads: "Let my people go free"?

CHAPTER EIGHTEENTH.

STEADY TRADES AND THEIR OUTLOOK.

"I USED to think there were steady trades; but somehow now everything gets mixed, and you can't tell what's steady and what isn't."

"What makes the mix?"

"The Lord only knows! I've studied over it till I'm dazed, and sometimes I've wondered if my mind was weakening."

The speaker, a middle-aged Scotchwoman, whose tongue still held a little of the burr that thirty years of American life had not been able to extract, put her hand to her head as if the fault must concentrate there.

"If it was my trade alone," she said, "I might think I was to blame for not learning new ways, but it's the same in all. Now, take mattress-making. I learned that because I could help my father best that way. He was an upholsterer in Aberdeen, and came over to better himself, and he did if he hadn't signed notes for a friend and ruined himself. He upholstered in the big families for thirty years, and everybody knew his little place on Hudson Street. People then bought furniture to last, and had it covered with the best of stuff, and so with curtains and hangings. Damask was damask, I can tell you, and velvet lambrequins meant money. No cotton-back stuff. They got shaken and brushed and done up from moths. People had some respect for good material. Nobody respects anything now. I saw a rich woman the other day let her boy six years old empty a box of candy on a pale-blue satin couch, and then sit down on it and rub his shoes up and down on the edge. I say that when there's no respect left for anything it's no wonder decent work comes to an end. I make a mattress and there isn't an inch of it that isn't sewed to last and that isn't an honest piece of work, but you can go into any house-furnishing department and buy one that looks just as well for a third less money. Everything's so cheap that people don't care whether anything lasts or not, and so there's no decent work done; and people pretend to have learned trades when really they just botch things together. I just go round in houses and make over,—places that I've had for years; and I've been forewoman in a big factory, but somehow a factory mattress never seems to me as springy and good as the old kind. Upholsterers make pretty good wages, but it can't be called steady any more, though it used to be. I've thought many a time of going into business for myself, but competition's awful, and I'm afraid to try. I won't cheat, and there's no getting ahead unless you do."

"What are the wages?"

"A picker gets about three dollars a week. She just picks over the hair, and most any kind of girl seems to do now that everything is steamed or done by machinery. The highest wages now are nine dollars a week, though I used to earn fifteen and eighteen sometimes, and the dull season makes the average about six dollars. I earn nine or ten because I do a good deal of private work, but a woman that can make forty dollars a month straight ahead is lucky."

Several women of much the same order of intelligence, two of them forewomen for years in prosperous establishments, added their testimony as to the shifting character of wages and of employments. One had watched the course of neckties for seventeen years,—a keen-eyed little widow who had fought hard to educate her two children and preserve some portion of the respectability she loved.

"You'd never dream how many kinds there have been, or, for that matter, how many kinds there are. We even make stocks for a few old-fashioned gentlemen that will have them. It's a business that a lady turns to first thing almost if she wants to earn, and we give out hundreds on hundreds to such, besides sending loads into the country. I often think our house turns out enough for the whole United States, but we're only a beginning. We pay well,—well as any, and better. Twenty-five cents a dozen is good pay now, and we see that our cutter leaves margin enough to keep the women from being cheated. That's a great trick with some. Sometimes the cutter is paid by the number he can get out of a piece of goods; sometimes he screws just because he's made so. But they cut by measure, and they allow so little to turn in that the thing frays in your hand, and no mortal could help it, and if one is frayed the foreman just throws out the dozen. Then lots of them advertise for girls to learn, and say they must give the first week or fortnight free; and when that is over they say work is slack or some other excuse, and take in a lot more that have been waiting. We've taken many a girl that came crying and told how she'd been kept on and cheated. There's one man on Third Avenue that runs his place on this plan, and has got rich. But I say to every girl: 'You'd better have something more than the last shape in neckties between you and starvation. You'll never get beyond five or six dollars a week at most, and generally not that.' It don't make any difference. There are dozens waiting for the chance to starve genteelly. It's a genteel trade and a pretty steady one, but if a dull time comes the girls go into cigar-making and manage along somehow. I've coaxed a good many into service, but it isn't one in a hundred will try that."

The third woman represented a hat-pressing factory in which she had been eleven years, and in which the wages had fallen year by year, till at present women, even when most expert, can earn not over six dollars per week as against from eight to twelve in previous years. The trade is regarded as a steady one, for spring and summer straws give place to felt, and a certain number of hands are sure of employment. In direct association with this trade must be considered that of artificial flowers and feathers, in which there is perpetual see-saw. If feathers are in vogue flowers are down, and *vice versa*. Five thousand women are employed on feathers, and the establishments, which in 1871 numbered but twelve, now number over fifty; but those for flowers far exceed them. Learners work for three dollars or less per week, the highest wages attainable in either being fifteen dollars, the average being about nine. The demand for one or the other is continuous, but when fashion in 1886 called for scarfs and flowers, four thousand feather-workers were thrown out and lived as they could till another turn in the wheel restored their occupation.

"One or the other of 'em is always steady" said a woman who had learned both trades, and thus stood prepared to circumvent fate. "The trouble is, you never know a week ahead which will be up and which down. Lots of us have learned both, and when I see the firm putting their heads together I know what it means and just go across the way to Pillsbury's, and the same with them. It's good pay and one or the other steady, but the Lord only knows which."

"If you want steadiness you've got to take to jute," said a girl who with her sister lived in one of the upper rooms. "There ain't many jute-mills in the country, and you go straight ahead. We two began in a cotton-mill, but there's this queer thing about it. Breathe cotton-fluff all day and you're just sure to have consumption; but breathe a peck of jute-fluff a day and it didn't seem to make any difference. That isn't my notion. Our doctor said he'd noticed it, and he took home some of the fibre to examine it. For my part we're called a rough lot, but I'd rather take that discredit and keep on in the mill. You can stir round and don't have to double up over sewing or that kind of thing. I can earn seven dollars a week, and I'd rather earn it that way than any other."

An hour or two in the mill, which included every form of manufacture that jute has yet taken, from seamless bags of all sizes and grades up to carpets, convinced one that if nerves were hardened to the incessant noise of machinery, there were distinct advantages associated with it. The few Scotch in the mill, men and women who had been brought over from Dundee, the headquarters of the jute industry abroad, insisted that jute was healthy, and long life for all who handled it a forgone conclusion. A tour among the workers seemed to confirm this impression, though here and there one found the factory face, with its dead paleness and dark-ringed eyes. Children as small as can be held to be consistent with the assumption of their thirteen years are preferred, their work as "doffers" or spool-changers requiring small quick hands. So, too, in fixing the pattern for carpets, where the threads must be manipulated with speed and light touch. It is preferred that children should grow up in the mill, passing from one room to another as they master processes, and the employees thus stay on and regard themselves as portions of the business. Some three or four thousand women and girls find occupation here. The waste from the carding-rooms is sent to the paper-mills and enters into manila paper and pasteboard, and this brings one to the paper-box makers, of whom there are several thousand at work.

This trade, while nominally one of the steadiest, has its short periods of depression. Competition is also as severe here as in every other present form of industry, and thus prices are kept down, the highest rate of wages earned being nine dollars, while seven dollars is considered fair. There must be a certain apprenticeship, not less than six months being required to master details and understand each stage of the work. In one of the best of these establishments, where space was plenty and ventilation and other conditions all good, one woman had been in the firm's employ for eighteen years and was practically forewoman, though no such office is recognized. Beginners were placed in her hands and did not leave her till a perfect box could be turned off. Cutting is all done by special machines, and the paper for covering is prepared in the same way, glue or paste being used according to the degree of strength desired in the box. The work is all piece-work, from fifty to seventy cents a hundred being paid; a fair worker making two hundred a day and an expert nearly or quite three hundred. But competition governs the price and cuts are often made. A firm will underbid and an order be transferred to it, unless the girls will consent to do the work five or, it may be, ten cents less on the hundred, and thus wages can seldom pass beyond nine dollars a week, dull seasons and cuts reducing the average to seven and a half. Many even good workers fall far below this, as they prefer to come late and go early, piece-work admitting of this arrangement. The woman who takes up this trade may be confident of earning from twenty-five to thirty-five dollars a month, but she never exceeds this amount; nor is there promotion beyond a certain point. In paper hangings wages do not rise above twenty-five dollars at most, and in paper collars and cuffs, as in everything connected with clothing, the rate is much less. Rags are the foundation industry in all these forms of paper manufacture, but the two thousand women who work at sorting these seldom pass beyond five dollars, and more often receive but two and a half or three dollars per week.

Under much the same head must come the preparation of sample cards, playing cards, and various forms of stationers' work. The latter has short dull seasons when girls may, for two or three weeks, have no work; but it is otherwise a steady trade, the wages running from three and a half to seven dollars per week. They stamp initials and crests with large hand presses, and stamp also the cheaper order of lithographs; they run envelope machines, color mourning paper, apply mucilage to envelopes, and pack small boxes of paper and envelopes. In all of the last mentioned trades hours are from eight A. M. to half-past five P. M., with half an hour for lunch, and a girl of fifteen can earn the same wages as the woman of fifty, a light, quick touch and care being the only essentials.

The trades mentioned here and in preceding papers form but a portion of the ninety and more open to women. Thirty-eight of these are directly connected with clothing, and include every phase of ornament or use in braid, gimp, button, clasp, lining, or other article employed in its manufacture. In every one of these competition keeps wages at the lowest possible figure. Outside of the army here employed come the washers and ironers who laundry shirts and underwear, whose work is of the most exhausting order, who "lean hard" on the iron, and in time become the victims of diseases resulting from ten hours a day of this "leaning hard," and who complain bitterly that prisons and reformatories underbid them and keep wages down. It is quite true. Convict labor here as elsewhere is the foe of the honest worker, and complicates a problem already sufficiently complicated. These ironers can make from ten to twelve dollars per week, but soon fail in health and turn to lighter work, many of them taking up cigar-making, which soon finishes the work of demoralization.

Fringes, gimps, plush, and bonnet ornaments are overcrowded with workers, for here, as in flowers and feathers, fashion determines the season's work, and the fringe-maker has for a year or so had small call for her knowledge save in some forms of upholstery. One and all are so hedged in by competition that to pass beyond a certain limit is impossible, and all wages are kept at the lowest point, not only by this fact, but by the fact that many women who had learned the trade continue it after marriage as a means of adding a trifle to the family income. An expert in any one of them is tolerably certain of steady employment, but wages have reached the lowest point and it does not appear that any rise is probable. Sharp competition rules and will rule till the working class themselves recognize the necessity of an education that will make them something more than adjuncts to machinery, and of an organization in which co-operation will take the place of competition. That both must come is as certain as that evolution is upward and not downward, but it is still a distant day, and neither employer nor employed have yet learned the possibilities of either.

CHAPTER NINETEENTH.

DOMESTIC SERVICE AND ITS PROBLEMS.

AT last we have come to the problem to which there has necessarily been incidental reference here and there, but which has otherwise bided its time. That these pages or any pages written by mortal hand in this generation can solve it, the writer doubts, its solution being inextricably involved with that of other social problems for which time is the chief key. State the question as we may, there is always a fresh presentation to be made, and replies are as various as the minds of the staters. It is the mistress with whom such presentation has thus far rested,—a mistress thorned beyond endurance by incompetence, dirt, waste, insubordination,—all the evils known to ignorant and presumptuous service. For such mistress, smarting from a sense of wrong, and hopeless and faithless as to remedies, the outlook is necessarily bounded by her own horizon. She listens with indignant contempt to the story of the thousands who choose their garrets and semi-starvation with independence, to the shelter and abundance of the homes in which they might be made welcome. She may even aver that any statement of their suffering is stupid sentimentality; the gush and maudlin melancholy of "humanitarian clergymen and newspaper reformers."

For her, as for most of her order, in whom as yet no faculty for seeing both sides of a question has developed, there can be no reply save in words already spoken. "These women, working for wages that keep them always just above starvation point, have no power left to think beyond the need of the hour. They cannot stop, they dare not stop, to think of other methods of earning. They have no clothing in which they could obtain even entrance to an intelligence office. They have no knowledge that could make them servants even of the meanest order. They are what is left of untrained and hopelessly ignorant lives," given over to suffering born in part from their ignorance; and for a large proportion of such cases there can be merely alleviation, and such slight bettering of conditions as would come from a system into which justice entered more fully.

With this army of incompetents we have at present nothing to do. Our interest lies in discovering what is at the bottom of the objection to domestic service; how far these objections are rational and to be treated with respect, and how they may be obviated. The mistress's point of view we all know. We know, too, her presentation of objections as she fancies she has discovered them. What we do not know is the ground taken by sensible, self-respecting girls, who have chosen trades in preference, and from whom full detail has been obtained as to the reasons for such choice. In listening to the countless stories of experiment in earning a living, the passage from one industry to another, and the uncertainties and despairs before the right thing had shown itself, the question has always been asked, "How did it happen that you did not try to get a place in some good family?"

The answers were as various as the characters of those who replied; some with indignation that they should be supposed capable of this degradation, but most of them thoughtfully and reasonably. In time they arranged themselves under heads, the occupations represented by the various respondents being over seventy. They were chiefly above the ordinary domestic in intelligence and education, their employments being of every order, from paper-box making to type-writing and stenography; but the trades predominated,—American being the nationality most largely represented, Irish born in this country ranking next, and German and a sprinkling of other nationalities following. These replies are precisely of the same nature as those given some time ago in Philadelphia during an investigation made by the head of one of the first guilds for working-women established in this country, objections being practically the same at whatever point they may be given. They were arranged under different heads and numbered in order.

In the present case it seems well to take the individual testimony, each girl whose verdict is chosen representing a class, and being really its mouthpiece.

First on the list stands Margaret M——, an American, twenty-three years old, and for five years in a paper-box factory. Seven others nodded their assent, or added a word here and there as she gave her view, two of them Irish-Americans who had had some years in the public schools.

"It's freedom that we want when the day's work is done. I know some nice girls, Bridget's cousins, that make more money and dress better and everything for being in service. They're waitresses, and have Thursday afternoon out and part of every other Sunday. But they're never sure of one minute that's their own when they're in the house. Our day is ten hours long, but when it's done it's done, and we can do what we like with the evenings. That's what I've heard from every nice girl that ever tried service. You're never sure that your soul's your own except when you are out of the house, and I couldn't stand that a day. Women care just as much for freedom as men do. Of course they don't get so much, but I know I'd fight for mine."

"Women are always harder on women than men are," said a fur-sewer, an intelligent American about thirty. "I got tired of always sitting, and took a place as chambermaid. The work was all right and the wages good, but I'll tell you what I couldn't stand. The cook and the waitress were just common, uneducated Irish, and I had to room with one and stand the personal habits of both, and the way they did at table took all my appetite. I couldn't eat, and began to run down; and at last I gave notice, and told the truth when I was asked why. The lady just looked at me astonished: 'If you take a servant's place, you can't expect to be one of the family,' she said. 'I never asked it,' I said; 'all I ask is a chance at common decency.' 'It will be difficult to find an easier place than this,' she said, and I knew it; but ease one way was hardness another, and she couldn't see that I had any right to complain. That's one trouble in the way. It's the mixing up of things, and mistresses don't think how they would feel in the same place."

Third came an Irish-American whose mother had been cook for years in one family, but who had, after a few months of service, gone into a jute-mill, followed gradually by five sisters.

"I hate the very words 'service' and 'servant,'" she said. "We came to this country to better ourselves, and it's not bettering to have anybody ordering you round."

"But you are ordered in the mill."

"That's different. A man knows what he wants, and doesn't go beyond it; but a woman never knows what she wants, and sort of bosses you everlastingly. If there was such a thing as fixed hours it might be different, but I tell every girl I know, 'Whatever you do, don't go into service. You'll always be prisoners and always looked down on.' You can do things at home for them as belongs to you that somehow it seems different to do for strangers. Anyway, I hate it, and there's plenty like me."

"What I minded," said a gentle, quiet girl, who worked at a stationer's, and who had tried household service for a year,—"what I minded was the awful lonesomeness. I went for general housework, because I knew all about it, and there were only three in the family. I never minded being alone evenings in my own room, for I'm always reading or something, and I don't go out hardly at all, but then I always know I can, and that there is somebody to talk to if I like. But there, except to give orders, they had nothing to do with me. It got to feel sort of crushing at last. I cried myself sick, and at last I gave it up, though I don't mind the work at all. I know there are good places, but the two I tried happened to be about alike, and I sha'n't try again. There are a good many would feel just the same."

"Oh, nobody need to tell me about poor servants," said an energetic woman of forty, Irish-American, and for years in a shirt factory. "Don't I know the way the hussies'll do, comin' out of a bog maybe, an' not knowing the names even, let alone the use, of half the things in the kitchen, and asking their twelve and fourteen dollars a month? Don't I know it well, an' the shame it is to 'em! but I know plenty o' decent, hard-workin' girls too, that give good satisfaction, an' this is what they say. They say the main trouble is, the mistresses don't know, no more than babies, what a day's work really is. A smart girl keeps on her feet all the time to prove she isn't lazy, for if the mistress finds her sitting down, she thinks there can't be much to do and that she doesn't earn her wages. Then if a girl tries to save herself or is deliberate, they call her slow. They want girls on tap from six in the morning till ten and eleven at night. 'Tisn't fair. And then, if there's a let-up in the work, maybe they give you the baby to see to. I like a nice baby, but I don't like having one turned over to me when I'm fit to drop scrabbling to get through and sit down a bit. I've naught to say for the girls that's breaking things and half doing the work. They're a shameful set, and ought to be put down somehow; but it's a fact that the most I've known in service have been another sort that stayed long in places and hated change. There's many a good place too, but the bad ones outnumber 'em. Women make hard mistresses, and I say again, I'd rather be under a man, that knows what he wants. That's the way with most."

"I don't see why people are surprised that we don't rush into places," said a shop-girl. "Our world may be a very narrow world, and I know it is; but for all that, it's the only one we've got, and right or wrong, we're out of it if we go into service. A teacher or cashier or anybody in a store, no matter if they have got common-sense, doesn't want to associate with servants. Somehow you get a sort of smooch. Young men think and say, for I have heard lots of them, 'Oh, she can't amount to much if she hasn't brains enough to make a living outside of a kitchen!' You're just down once for all if you go into one."

"I don't agree with you at all," said a young teacher who had come with her. "The people that hire you go into kitchens and are not disgraced. What I felt was, for you see I tried it, that they oughtn't to make me go into livery. I was worn out with teaching, and so I concluded to try being a nurse for a while. I found two hard things: one, that I was never free for an hour from the children, for I took meals and all with them, and any mother knows what a rest it is to go quite away from them, even for an hour; and the other was that she wanted me to wear the nurse's cap and apron. She was real good and kind; but when I said, 'Would you like your sister, Miss Louise, to put on cap and apron when she goes out with them?' she got very red, and straightened up. 'It's a very different matter,' she said; 'you must not forget that in accepting a servant's place you accept a servant's limitations.' That finished me. I loved the children, but I said, 'If you have no other thought of what I am to the children than that, I had better go.' I went, and she put a common, uneducated Irish girl in my place. I know a good many who would take nurse's places, and who are sensible enough not to want to push into the family life. But the trouble is that almost every one wants to make a show, and it is more stylish to have the nurse in a cap and apron, and so she is ordered into them."

"I've tried it," said one who had been a dressmaker and found her health going from long sitting. "My trouble was, no conscience as to hours; and I believe you'll find that is, at the bottom, one of the chief objections. My first employer was a smart, energetic woman, who had done her own work when she was first married and knew what it meant, or you'd think she might have known. But she had no more thought for me than if I had been a machine. She'd sit in her sitting-room on the second floor and ring for me twenty times a day to do little things, and she wanted me up till eleven to answer the bell, for she had a great deal of company. I had a good room and everything nice, and she gave me a great many things, but I'd have spared them all if only I could have had a little time to myself. I was all worn out, and at last I had to go. There was another reason. I had no place but the kitchen to see my friends. I was thirty years old and as well born and well educated as she, and it didn't seem right. The mistresses think it's all the girls' fault, but I've seen enough to know that women haven't found out what justice means, and that a girl knows it, many a time, better than her employer. Anyway, you couldn't make me try it again."

"My trouble was," said another, who had been in a cotton-mill and gone into the home of one of the mill-owners as chambermaid, "I hadn't any place that I could be alone a minute. We were poor at home, and four of us worked in the mill, but I had a little room all my own, even if it didn't hold much. In that splendid big house the servants' room was over the kitchen,—hot and close in summer, and cold in winter, and four beds in it. We five had to live there together, with only two bureaus and a bit of a closet, and one washstand for all. There was no chance to keep clean or your things in nice order, or anything by yourself, and I gave up. Then I went into a little family and tried general housework, and the mistress taught me a great deal, and was good and kind, only there the kitchen was a dark little place and my room like it, and I hadn't an hour in anything that was pleasant and warm. A mistress might see, you'd think, when a girl was quiet and fond of her home, and treat her different from the kind that destroy everything; but I suppose the truth is, they're worn out with that kind and don't make any difference. It's hard to give up your whole life to somebody else's orders, and always feel as if you was looked at over a wall like; but so it is, and you won't get girls to try it, till somehow or other things are different."

Last on the record came a young woman born in Pennsylvania in a fairly well-to-do farmer's house.

"I like house-work," she said. "There's nothing suits me so well. We girls never had any money, nor mother either, and so I went into a water-cure near the Gap and stayed awhile. Now the man that run it believed in all being one family. He called the girls helpers, and he fixed things so't each one had some time to herself every day, and he tried to teach 'em all sorts of things. The patients were cranky to wait on, but you felt as if you was a human being, anyhow, and had a chance. Well, I watched things, and I said it was discouraging, sure enough. I tried to do a square day's work, but two-thirds of 'em there shirked whenever they could; half did things and then lied to cover their tracks. I was there nine months, and I learned better'n ever I knew before how folks ought to live on this earth. And I said to myself the fault wasn't so much in the girls that hadn't ever been taught; it was in them that didn't know enough to teach 'em. A girl thought it was rather pretty and independent, and showed she was somebody, to sling dishes on the table, and never say 'ma'am' nor 'sir,' and dress up afternoons and make believe they hadn't a responsibility on earth. They hadn't sense enough to do anything first-rate, for nobody had ever put any decent ambition into 'em. It isn't to do work well; it's to get somehow to a place where there won't be any more work. So I say that it's the way of living and thinking that's all wrong; and that as soon as you get it ciphered out and plain before you that any woman, high or low, is a mean sneak that doesn't do everything in the best way she can possibly learn, and that doesn't try to help everybody to feel just so, why, things would stop being crooked and folks would get along well enough. Don't you think so?"

How far the energetic speaker had solved the problem must be left to the reader, for whom there still certain unconsidered phases, all making part of the arraignment, scouted by those who are served, but more and more distinct and formidable in the mind of the server.

CHAPTER TWENTIETH.

MORE PROBLEMS OF DOMESTIC SERVICE.

THOUGH the testimony given in the preceding chapter on this topic includes the chief objection to be made by the class of workers who would seem to be most benefited by accepting household service, there remain still one or two phases seldom mentioned, but forming an essential portion of the argument against it. They belong, not to the order we have had under consideration, but to that below it from which the mass of domestic servants is recruited, and with which the housekeeper must most often deal.

The phases encountered here are born of the conditions of life in the cities and large towns; and denied as they may be by quiet householders whose knowledge of life is bounded by their own walls, or walls enclosing neighbors of like mind, they exist and face at once all who look below the surface. The testimony of the class itself might be open to doubt. The testimony of the physicians whose work lies among them, or in the infirmaries to which they come, cannot be impugned. Shirk or deny facts as we may, it is certain that in the great cities, save for the comparatively small proportion of quiet homes where old methods still prevail, household service has become synonymous with the worst degradation that comes to woman. Women who have been in service, and remained in it contentedly until marriage, unite in saying that things have so changed that only here and there is a young girl safe, and that domestic service is the cover for more licentiousness than can be found in any other trade in which women are at work.

Incredible as this statement at first appears, the statistics of hospitals and in infirmaries confirm it, and the causes are not far to seek. Household service has passed from the hands of Americans into those of the Irish first, and then a proportion of every European nation. So long as the supply came to us entirely from abroad we were comparatively safe. If the experience of the new arrival had been solely under thatched roof and on clay floors, at least sun could visit them and great chimneys gave currents of pure air, while simple food kept blood pure and gave small chance for unruly impulses to govern. But once with us demoralization began, and the tenement-house guaranteed sure corruption for every tenant. Even for the most decent there was small escape. To the children born in these quarters every inmost fact of human life was from the beginning a familiar story. Overcrowding, the impossibility of slightest privacy, the constant contact with the grossest side of life, soon deaden any susceptibility and destroy every gleam of modesty or decency. In the lowest order of all rules an absolute shamelessness which conceals itself in the grade above, yet has no less firm hold of those who have come up in such conditions.

There are many exceptions, many well-fought battles against their power, but our concern at present is not with these but with facts as they stand recorded. Physician after physician has given in her testimony and one and all agree in the statement that open prostitution is for many merely the final step,—a mere setting the seal to the story of ruin and licentiousness that has always existed. The women who adopt this mode of life because of want of work or low wages are the smallest of minorities. The illegitimate children for whom the city must care are not from this source. Often the mother is a mere child who has been deceived and outraged, but far more often she has entered a family prepared to meet any advances, and often directly the tempter.

It is this state of things which makes many mothers say: "My girl shall never run such risks. I'll keep her from them as long as I can;" and unsavory as the details will seem, their knowledge is an essential factor in the problem. The tenement-house stands to-day not only as the breeder of disease and physical degeneration for every inmate, but as equally potent in social demoralization for the class who ignore its existence. Out of these houses come hundreds upon hundreds of our domestic servants, whose influence is upon our children at the most impressible age, and who bring inherited and acquired foulness into our homes and lives. And if such make but the smallest proportion of those who serve, they are none the less powerful and most formidable agents in that blunting of moral perception which is a more and more apparent fact in the life of the day. The records from which such knowledge is gleaned are not accessible to the general public. They are formulated only by the physician, whose business is silence, and who gives only an occasional summary of what may be found in the sewer underlying the social life of great cities. Decorously hidden from view the foul stream flows on, rising here and there to the surface, but instantly covered by popular opinion, which pronounces such revelations disgusting and considers suppression synonymous with extermination.

Naturally this phase of things is confined chiefly to the great cities, but the virus is portable and its taint may be discovered even in the remote country. It is one of the many causes that have worked toward the degradation of this form of service, but it is so interwoven and integral a part of the present social structure that temporary destruction would seem the inevitable result of change. Yet change must come before the only class who have legitimate place in our homes will or can take such place. If different ideals had ruled among us; if ease and freedom from obligation and "a good time" had not come to be the chief end of man to-day; if our schools gave any training from which boy or girl could go out into life with the best in them developed and ready for actual practical use,—this mass of undisciplined, conscienceless, reckless force would have been reduced to its lowest terms, and to dispose of the residuum would be an easy problem. As it is, we are at the mercy of the spirits we have raised, and no one word holds power to lay them. No axioms or theories of the past have any present application. It is because we cling to the old theories while diligently practising methods in absolute opposition to them, that the question has so complicated itself. We cannot go backward, but we can stop short and discover in what direction our path is tending and whether we are not wandering blindly in by-ways, when the public road is clear to see.

It is certain that many among the most intelligent working-women look longingly toward domestic service as something that might offer much more individual possibility of comfort and contentment than the trades afford. But save for one here and there who has chanced to find an employer who knows the meaning of justice as well as of human sympathy, the mass turn away hopeless of any change in methods. Yet reform among intelligent employers could easily be brought about were the question treated from the standpoint of justice, and the demand made an equally imperative and binding one for each side. The mistresses who command the best service are those who make rigorous demands, but keep their own side of the bargain as rigorously. They are few, for the American temperament is one of submission, varied by sudden bursts of revolt, and despairing return to a worse state than the first. A training-school school for mistresses is as much an essential as one for the servants. The conditions of modern life come more complicated with every year; and as simplification becomes for the many less and less possible, it is all the more vitally necessary to study the subject from the new standpoint, settle once for all how and why we have failed, and begin again on the new foundation.

Here then stands the arraignment of domestic service under its present conditions, given point by point as it has formulated itself to those who urged to turn to it. The mistresses' side defines itself as sharply; but when all is said the two are one, the demand one and the same for both. Men who work for wages work a specified number of hours, and if they shirk or half fulfil their contract, find work taken from them. Were the same arrangement understood as equally binding in domestic service, thousands of self-respecting women would not hesitate to enter it. Family life cannot always move in fixed lines, and hours must often vary; but conscientious tally could be kept, and over-hours receive the pay they have earned. A conscience on both sides would be the first necessity; and it is quite certain that the master of the house would require education as decidedly as the mistress, woman's work within home walls being regarded as something continuous, indefinable, and not worth formal estimate.

In spite of the enormous increase of wealth, the mass are happily what, for want of a better word, must be called middle class. But one servant or helper can usually be kept, and most often she is one who has used our kitchens as kindergartens, adding fragments of training as she passed from one to the other, ending often as fairly serviceable and competent. Sure of her place she becomes tyrant, and nothing can alter this relation but the appearance upon the scene of organized trained labor, making a demand for absolute fairness of treatment and giving it in return. Once certain that the reign of incompetence was over, the present order of servers would make haste to seek training-schools, or accept the low wages which would include personal training from the mistress, promotion being conditioned upon faithful obedience to the new order.

What are the stipulations which every self-respecting girl or woman has the right to make? They are short and simple. They are absolutely reasonable, and their adoption would be an education to every household which accepted them:—

1. A definition of what a day's work means, and payment for all over-time required, or certain hours of absolute freedom guaranteed, especially where the position is that of child's nurse.

2. A comfortably warmed and decently furnished room, with separate beds if two occupy it, and both decent place and appointments for meals.

3. The heaviest work, such as carrying coal, scrubbing pavements, washing, etc., to be arranged for if this is asked, with a consequent deduction in the wages.

4. No livery if there is feeling against it.

5. The privilege of seeing friends in a better part of the house than the kitchen, and security from any espionage during such time, whether the visitors are male or female. This to be accompanied by reasonable restrictions as to hours, and with the condition that work is not to be neglected.

6. Such a manner of speaking to and of the server as shall show that there is no contempt for housework, and that it is actually as respectable as other occupations.

Were such a schedule as this printed, framed, and hung in every kitchen in the land, and its provisions honestly met, household revolution and anarchy would cease, and the whole question settle itself quietly and once for all. And this in spite of a thousand inherent difficulties known to every housekeeper, but which would prove self-adjusting so soon as it was learned that service had found a rational basis. At present, with the majority of mistresses, it is simply unending struggle to get the most out of the unwilling and grudging server, hopelessly unreasonable and giving warning on faintest provocation. Yet these very women, turning to factory life, where fixed and inexorable law rules with no appeal, submit at once and become often skilled and capable workers. It is certain that domestic service must learn organization as every other form of industry has learned it, and that mistresses must submit to something of the same training that is needed by the maid. Nor need it be feared that putting such service on a strictly business basis will destroy such kindliness as now helps to make the relation less intolerable. On the contrary, with justice the foundation and a rigorous fulfilment of duty on both sides will come a far closer tie than exists save in rarest instances, and homes will regain a quality long ago vanished from our midst. Such training will be the first step toward the co-operation which must be the ultimate solution of many social problems.

It has failed in many earlier attempts because personal justice was lacking; but even one generation of sustained effort to simplify conditions would insure not only a different ideal for those who think at all, but the birth of something better for every child of the Republic.

For the individual standing alone, hampered by many cares and distracted over the whole household problem, action may seem impossible. But if the most rational members of a community would band together, send prejudice and tradition to the winds, and make a new declaration of independence for the worker, it is certain that the tide would turn and a new order begin. Till such united, concerted action can be brought about there is small hope of reform, and it can come only through women. Dismiss sentiment. Learn to look at the thing as a trade in which each seeks her own advantage, and in which each gains the more clearly these advantages are defined. It is a hard relation. It demands every power that woman can bring to bear upon it. It is an education of the highest faculties she owns. It means a double battle, for it is with ourselves that the fight begins. Liberty can only come through personal struggle. It is easy to die for it, but to live for it, to deserve it, to defend it forever is another and a harder matter. Still harder is it to know its full meaning and what it is that makes the battle worth fighting. Union to such ends will be slow, but it must come:—

> "Freedom is growth and not creation:
> One man suffers, one man is free.
> One brain forges a constitution,

But how shall the million souls be won?
Freedom is more than a revolution—
He is not free who is free alone."

Is this the word of a dreamer whose imagination holds the only work of reconstruction, and whose hands are powerless to make the dream reality? On the contrary, many years of experience in which few of the usual troubles were encountered, added to that of others who had thought out the problem for themselves, have demonstrated that reform is possible. Precisely such conditions as are here specified have been in practical operation for many years. The homes in which they have ruled have had the unfailing devotion of those who served, and the experiment has ceased to come under that head, and demonstrated that order and peace and quiet mastery of the day's work may still be American possessions. Count this imperfect presentation then as established fact for a few, and ask why it is not possible to make it so for the many.

CHAPTER TWENTY-FIRST.

END AND BEGINNING.

THE long quest is over. It ends; and I turn at last from those women, whose eyes still follow me, filled with mute question of what good may come. Of all ages and nations and creeds, all degrees of ignorance and prejudice and stupidity; hampered by every condition of birth and training; powerless to rise beyond them till obstacles are removed,—the great city holds them all, and in pain and want and sorrow they are one. The best things of life are impossible to them. What is worse, they are unknown as well as unattainable. If the real good of life must be measured by the final worth of the thing we make or get by it, what worth is there for or in them? The city holds them all,—"the great foul city,—rattling, growling, smoking, stinking,—a ghastly heap of fermenting brickwork, pouring out poison at every pore."

The prosperous have no such definition, nor do they admit that it can be true. For the poor, it is the only one that can have place. We pack them away in tenements crowded and foul beyond anything known even to London, whose "Bitter Cry" had less reason than ours; and we have taken excellent care that no foot of ground shall remain that might mean breathing-space, or free sport of child, or any green growing thing. Grass pushes its way here and there, but for this army it is only something that at last they may lie under, never upon. There is no pause in the march, where as one and another drops out the gap fills instantly, every alley and by-way holding unending substitutes. It is not labor that profiteth, for body and soul are alike starved. It is labor in its basest, most degrading form; labor that is curse and never blessing, as true work may be and is. It blinds the eyes. It steals away joy. It blunts all power whether of hope or faith. It wrecks the body and it starves the soul. It is waste and only waste; nor can it, below ground or above, hold fructifying power for any human soul.

Here then we face them,—ignorant, blind, stupid, incompetent in every fibre,—and yet no count of such indictment alters our responsibility toward them. Rather it multiplies it in always increasing ratio. For it is our own system that has made these lives worthless, and sooner or later we must answer how it came, that living in a civilized land they had less chance than the heathen to whom we send our missionaries, and upon whose occasional conversions we plume ourselves as if thus the Kingdom of Heaven were made wider. If it is true that for many only a little alleviation is possible, a little more justice, a little better apportionment of such good as they can comprehend, it is also true that something better is within the reach of all.

How then shall we define it, and what possibility of alteration for either lives or conditions lies before us? Nothing that can be of instant growth; and here lies the chief discouragement, since as a people we demand instantaneousness, and would have seed, flower, and fruit at the same moment. Admit patience, capacity to wait, and to work while waiting, as the first term of the equation, and the rest arrange themselves.

For the greater part of social reformers, co-operation has stood as the initial and most essential step, as the fruit that could be plucked full-grown; and experience in England would seem to have demonstrated the belief as true. It is the American inability to wait that has proved it untrue for us, and until very lately made failure our only record; but there is a deeper reason than a merely temperamental one. The abolition of the apprentice system, brought about by the greed of master and men alike, has abolished training and slow, steady preparation for any trade. An American has been regarded as quick enough and keen enough to take in the essential features of a calling, as it were, at a glance, and apprenticeship has been taken as practically an insult to national intelligence. Law has kept pace with such conviction, and thus the door has been shut in the face of all learners, and foreigners have supplied our skilled workmen and work-women. The groundwork of any better order lies, if not in a return to the apprentice system, then in a training from the beginning, which will give to eye and hand the utmost power of which they are capable. Industrial education is the foundation, and until it has in its broadest and deepest sense become the portion of every child born on American soil, that child has missed its birthright.

With the many who accept it, it stands merely as an added capacity to make money, and if taken in its narrowest application this is all that it can do. Were this all, it would be simply an added injustice toward the degeneration that money-making for the mere sake of money inevitably brings. But at its best, perfected as it has been by patient effort on the part of a few believers, it is far more than this. Added power to earn comes with it, but there comes also a love of the work itself, such as has had no place since the days when the great guilds gave joyfully their few hours daily to the cathedrals, whose stones were laid and cemented in love and hope, and a knowledge of the beauty to come, that long ago died out of any work the present knows. The builders had small book knowledge. They could be talked down by any public-school child in its second or third year. But they knew the meaning of beauty and order and law; and this trinity stands to-day, and will stand for many a generation to come, as an ideal to which we must return till like causes work again to like ends. The child who could barely read saw beauty on every side, and took in the store of ballad and tradition that gave life to labor. We have parted with all this wilfully. To the Puritan all beauty that hand of man could create was of the devil, and thus we represent a consecrated ugliness, any departure from which is even now, by some conscientious souls, regarded with suspicion.

The child, then, who can be made to understand that beauty and order and law are one, has a new sense born in him. Life takes on a new aspect, and work a new meaning. But the fourteen weeks per year of education, at present required by our law as it stands in its application to children who must work, has no power to bring such result. It begins in the kindergarten, from which the poorest child takes home, even to the tenement-house, something strong enough, when growth has come, to abolish the tenement-house forever. No man who works to these ends has gauged possibilities more wisely than Felix Adler, whose school shows us something not yet attained by the many who, partially accepting his methods, pronounce his theories dangerous and destructive to what must be held sacred. However this may be, he and his band of co-workers have proved, in seven years of unceasing struggle against heavy odds, that a development is possible even for the tenement-house child, that reconstructs the entire view of life and makes possible the end for which all industrial training is but the preparation. It is in such training that children, rich or poor, best learn the demand bound up in living and working together, and find in the end that co-operation is its natural out-growth. There is no renunciation of the home or destruction of the truest home life. There is simply the abolition of competition as any necessary factor in human progress, and the placing of the worker beyond its power to harm.

Thus far we have left the bettering of social conditions chiefly to the individual, and any hint of State interference carries with it the opprobrium of socialism. Yet more and more for those who are unterrified by names, the best in socialism offers itself as the sole way of escape from monopolies and the stupidities and outrages of the present system. No one panacea of any reformer fits the case or can alter existing conditions. Only what man's own soul sees as good, and wills to possess, is of faintest value to him. No attempt at co-operation can help till the worker sees its power and use, and is willing to sacrifice where sacrifice is necessary, to work and to wait in patience. Such power is born in the industrial school in its largest sense,— the school that trains heart and mind as well eye and hand, and makes the child ready for the best work its measure of power can know. This we can give by State or by individual aid, as the case may be, and every ward in the city should own a sufficient number to include every child within it. A check upon emigration would seem an imperative demand,—not prevention, but some clause which might act to lessen the garbage-heaps dumped upon our shores. Pauperism and disease have no rights as emigrants, and eliminating these would make dealing with mere poverty a much more manageable matter.

The schools exist, and, while painfully inadequate in number, demonstrate what may be done in the future. Co-operation even for this hasty people is almost equally demonstrated, as will be plain to those who read two recent publications of the American Economic Association: "Co-operation in a Western City," by Albert Shaw, and "Co-operation in New England," by Edward W. Bemis. Minneapolis is the centre of the facts given in the first-mentioned pamphlet, which is also the more valuable of the two, not in execution but merely because it records a movement which has ceased to be experimental; as the little history includes every failure as well as the final success, and thus stands as the best argument yet made for the cause.

Industrial education for the child of to-day; co-operation as the end to be attained by the worker into which the child will grow,—in these two factors is bound up much of the problem. They will not touch many whose miserable lives are recorded in these pages, but they will forever end any chance of another generation in like case. There are workers who think, who are being educated by sharp conflict with circumstances, and who look beyond their own present need to the future. These men and women, crowded to the wall by the present system, are searching eagerly, not as mere anarchists and destroyers, but as those who believe that something better than destruction is possible.

It is these workers for whom the path must be made plain, and to whom we are most heavily responsible. And this brings me to the final point bound up indissolubly with the two already defined,—a change in our own ideals. Such change must come before any school can accomplish its best work, and till it has at least begun neither school nor system has lasting power. In these months of search in which women of all ages and grades have given in their testimony,—from the girl of fourteen earning her two or three dollars a week in the bag-factory or as cash-girl, to the woman stitching her remnant of life into the garments that by and by her more fortunate sisters will find on the bargain counter,—I discover not alone their ignorance and stupidity and grossness and wilful blindness, but behind it an ignorance and stupidity no less dense upon which theirs is founded,— our own. The visible wretchedness is so appalling, the need for instant relief so pressing, that it is small wonder that no power remains to look beyond the moment, or to disentangle one's self from the myriad conflicting claims, and ask the real meaning of the demand. Mile after mile of the fair islands once the charm of the East River and the great Sound beyond are covered by lazar-houses,—the visible signs in this great equation that fills the page of to-day; the problem of human crime and disease and wretchedness complicating itself with every addition, and no nearer solution than when the city was but a handful of houses and poverty yet unknown.

We have made attempts here and there to limit the breeding ground; to offer less fruitful soil to the spawn increasing with such frightful rapidity, and demanding with every year fresh reformatories, larger asylums and hospitals, more and more machinery of alleviation. Yet the conviction strengthens that even when the tenement-house of to-day is swept aside, and improved homes with decent sanitary conditions have taken their place, that the root of the evil is even then untouched, and that it lies not alone in their lives, but in our own. And so, as final word, I say to-day to all women who give their lives to beneficence, and plan ceaselessly and untiringly for better days, that no beneficence can alter, no work of our hands or desire of our hearts bring the better day we desire, till the foundations have been laid in something less shifting than the sands on which we build.

The mission of alleviation, of protection, of care for the foulest and lowest of lives, has had its day. It is time that this mass of effort stirred against its perpetual reproduction, its existence, its ever more and more shameless demands. An improved home goes far toward making these tendencies less strong; it may even diminish the number of actual transgressors; but what home, no matter how well kept, has or will have power to alter the fact that in them thousands of women must still slave for a pittance that borders always on that life limit fixed by the political economists as the vanishing point in the picture of modern life? Sunlight and air may take the place of the foulness now reigning in the dens that many of them know as homes; but will either sun or air shorten hours or raise wages, or alter the fact that not one in a thousand of these women but has grounded her whole pitiful life on a delusion,—a delusion for which we are responsible?

Year by year in the story of the Republic, labor has taken lower and lower place. The passion for getting on, latent in every drop of American blood, has made money the sole symbol of success, and freedom from hand-labor the synonyme of happiness. The mass of illiterate, unenlightened emigrants pouring in a steady stream through Castle Garden have become our hands, and, as hands dependent on the heads of others, have fallen into the same category as the slaves, whose possession brought infinitely more degradation to owners than to owned. It is the story of every civilized nation before its fall,—this exploitation of labor, this degradation of the worker; and the story of hopeless decay and collapse must be ours also, if different ideals do not rise to fill the place of this Golden Calf to which all have bent the knee. There is not a girl old enough to work at all who does not dream of a possible future in which work will cease and ease and luxury take its place. The boy content with a trade, the man or woman accepting simple living and its limitations contentedly, is counted fool. To get money, and always more and more money, is the one ambition; and in this mad rush toward the golden fountain, gentle virtues are trampled under foot, and men count no armor of honest thought worth wearing unless it be fringed with bullion. The shop-girl must have her cotton velvet and her glass substitutes for diamonds. The lines of caste are drawn as sharply with her as in the ascending grades through which she hopes to pass. Labor is curse; never the blessing that it may bear when accepted man's chief good, and used as developing, not as destroying power.

Never till men see and believe that the fortune made by mere sharpness and unscrupulousness, the fruit not of honest labor but of pure speculation, is a burning disgrace to its owner, a plague-spot in civilization, shall we be able to convince girl or woman that labor is honorable, and better gains possible than any involved in merely getting on. Never till this furious fight for success, this system of competition which kills all regard for the individual, demanding only a machine capable of so much net product,— never till these and all methods of like nature have ceased to have place, or right to existence, can we count ourselves civilized or hope to better the conditions that now baffle us. No church, no mission, no improved home, no guild or any other form of mitigation means anything till the whole system of thought is reconstructed, and we come to some sense of what the eternal verities really are.

It is easy for a woman to be kind and long-suffering, but the women who can be just to themselves, as well as to others, we can count on our fingers. Yet justice is the one demand in this life of to-day, and not one of us who shrinks and shudders at the thought of what women-workers are enduring but has it in her power to lessen the great sum of wretchedness; to begin for some one the work of education into just thinking and just living. Sweeping changes may not be possible. But beginning is always possible; and not a woman capable of thinking but has power by the simple force of example to lay the corner-stone of the new temple, fairer than any yet known to mortal eyes. If there is doubt for this generation of working-women toiling in blindest ignorance, it rests with us to lessen the doubt for the next, and to make it impossible in that better day for which we labor. Not one of us but can ask, "What is the source of the income which gives me ease? Is it possible for me to reconstruct my own life in such fashion that it shall mean more direct and personal relation to the worker? How can I bring more simplicity, less conventionality, more truth and right living into home and every relation of life?"

I write these final words with all deference to the noble women whose lives have been given to good work, and many of whom long ago settled these questions practically for themselves. But for many of us there has been simply passive acceptance of all present conditions, without a question as to how or why they have come. It is because I believe that with us is the power to remedy every one if we will, that I appeal to women to-day. I write not as anarchist; not as declaimer against the rights of property, but as believer in the full right to ownership of all legitimately acquired property. I believe it the order of life, of any life that would hold good work of whatever nature, that enough should be acquired to make sharp want or eating care and perplexity impossible. But it is certain that even for the most unselfish of us there is an exaggerated estimate of the value of money,—an involuntary and inevitable truckling to the one who has most,—and that, no matter what our teaching may be, the force of every act and tendency makes against it. And there can be no retracing of steps that have for generations turned in the wrong direction. The very breath we draw on this American soil is poisoned by the foulness about us, and about us by our own act and choice. We have degraded labor till there is no lower depth, and not one but many generations must pass before these masses over whose condition we puzzle can find their feet in the path that means any real progress.

Ask first, then, not what shall we do for these women, but what shall we do for ourselves? How shall we learn to know what are the real things? How shall we come to love them and cleave to them, and hold no life worth living that admits sham or compromise, or believes the mad luxury of this generation anything but blighting curse and surest destruction? Till we know this we have learned nothing, and are forever not helpers, but hinderers, in the great march that our blunders and stupidities only check for the time. For the word is forever onward, and even the blindest soul must one day see that if he will not walk by free choice in the path of God, he will be driven into it with whips of scorpions, made thus to know what part was given him to fill, and what judgment waits him who has chosen blindness.

Milton Keynes UK
Ingram Content Group UK Ltd.
UKHW040816051024
449151UK00004B/272